The
Inspirational
Leader

How to motivate, encourage
and achieve success

JOHN ADAIR

**KOGAN
PAGE**

London and Philadelphia

Publisher's note

Every possible effort has been made to ensure that the information contained in this book is accurate at the time of going to press, and the publishers and authors cannot accept responsibility for any errors or omissions, however caused. No responsibility for loss or damage occasioned to any person acting, or refraining from action, as a result of the material in this publication can be accepted by the editor, the publisher or any of the authors.

First published in Great Britain and the United States in 2003 by Kogan Page Limited.
Reprinted 2004
Paperback edition 2005
Reprinted 2006, 2008
This edition 2009

Apart from any fair dealing for the purposes of research or private study, or criticism or review, as permitted under the Copyright, Designs and Patents Act 1988, this publication may only be reproduced, stored or transmitted, in any form or by any means, with the prior permission in writing of the publishers, or in the case of reprographic reproduction in accordance with the terms and licences issued by the CLA. Enquiries concerning reproduction outside these terms should be sent to the publishers at the undermentioned addresses:

Kogan Page Limited
120 Pentonville Road
London N1 9JN
United Kingdom
www.koganpage.com

Kogan Page US
525 South 4th Street, #241
Philadelphia PA 19147
USA

© John Adair, 2003, 2009

The right of John Adair to be identified as the author of this work has been asserted by him in accordance with the Copyright, Designs and Patents Act 1988.

ISBN 978 0 7494 5478 4

British Library Cataloguing-in-Publication Data

A CIP record for this book is available from the British Library.

Library of Congress Cataloging-in-Publication Data

Adair, John Eric, 1934–
    The inspirational leader : how to motivate, encourage and achieve success / John Adair.
        p. cm.
    Includes bibliographical references.
    ISBN 978-0-7494-5478-4
    1. Leadership. I. Title.
HD57.7.A275 2009
658.4'092 – dc22
                                                    2008042294

Typeset by Saxon Graphics Ltd, Derby
Printed and bound in India by Replika Press Pvt Ltd

Blackburn
College

Library
01254 292120

JOHN ADAIR is now widely regarded as the world's leading authority on leadership and leadership development. The author of 30 books on the subject, he has been named as one of the 40 people worldwide who have contributed most to the development of management thought and practice.

Educated at St Paul's School, London, John Adair has enjoyed a varied and colourful career. He served as adjutant in a Bedouin regiment in the Arab Legion, worked as a deckhand on an Arctic trawler and had a spell as an orderly in a hospital operating theatre. After Cambridge he became Senior Lecturer in Military History and Leadership Training Adviser at the Royal Military Academy, Sandhurst, before becoming the first Director of Studies at St George's House in Windsor Castle and then Associate Director of the Industrial Society. Later he became the world's first Professor in Leadership Studies at the University of Surrey. He also helped to found Europe's first Centre for Leadership Studies at the University of Exeter.

John now acts as a national and international adviser on leadership development. His recent books, published by Kogan Page, include *Not Bosses but Leaders*, *The Inspirational Leader*, *How to Grow Leaders* and *Leadership and Motivation*.

Contents

Introduction

'What can I do to help?' I asked the young chief executive. Over a cup of coffee he explained to me that he had read some books on leadership, and attended some courses, and that he had found them both valuable and useful in his path to becoming a leader. But now he felt that he had come up against a roadblock which prevented him from meeting the real challenges in his present role as a strategic leader. 'I feel that I lack the competence and confidence to be an *inspiring* leader,' he said. 'Can you help me to develop the charisma I need?'

'To be honest, I don't know if I can or not,' I replied. 'Certainly I know there is no such thing as instant inspirational leadership. There are no magic bullets. All I can suggest is that we explore together the nature and practice of leadership, and see what, if anything, we may discover that will help you in your quest to realize the potential within you. I can promise you no results, but plenty of hard thinking. Would that appeal to you?'

'That would be great,' he replied. 'When can we start?'

Over the following weeks and months our discussions, as you will see, ranged widely – from the principles of leadership in general to particular problems the young chief executive had encountered as a leader, some of the issues he faced today at work, and his hopes and fears for the future. In editing our conversations for publication, doing my best to preserve their flavour, I found our meetings both instructive and enjoyable. When I had finished the written draft I asked him to check it, and he made a number of useful suggestions from his perspective. So here you have the essence of our discussions.

What prompted me most to publish these conversations was seeing the change that had occurred in the young chief executive. 'As a result of talking with you,' he said, 'I now feel a lot more confident that I won't let people down if I am their leader, that I'll really be able to encourage and inspire them. And,' he added, 'I have a lot more faith and confidence in myself and the future.' He also said that he had immensely valued the opportunity to explore ideas about leadership; it had been great fun, and he had learned a lot.

At various points in our discussions, when either the young chief executive or I suggested it, we paused to capture on a flip chart some of the key points that had emerged. Afterwards he mentioned these as being especially helpful as an *aide-mémoire*. Apparently he kept them on his laptop and referred back to them whenever he had a few spare moments in the week. I hope that they will be equally useful as a means of refreshing your memory if you choose also to follow the 'steep and thorny path' signposted below to becoming an inspiring leader. As you make your way forwards, however, slow your steps, remember that:

> There is no failure except in no longer trying. There is no defeat except from within, no insurmountable barrier except our own inherent weakness of purpose.

Not Geniuses, But Average Men And
Women Require Profound Stimulation,
Incentive Towards Creative Effort,
And The Nurture of Great Hopes

Part 1

The Three Basic Approaches

The young chief executive began with a question. 'I have been thinking about your point,' he said, 'that there are no short cuts, no easy solutions to becoming an inspiring leader. Are you trying to tell me in a gentle way that it is quite impossible – if you are not a born leader it is too late?'

'Not impossible,' I countered, 'but it is not easy. Otherwise I suppose a lot more managers today would be good leaders. Perhaps we all inspire others once or twice in our careers. But inspiring others is a bit like getting a hole-in-one at golf: doing it once is just a lucky fluke, and many players pull it off once in their golfing career, but to come near to doing it all the time suggests that you have mastered the art of golf.'

'Are you saying that learning to inspire others can be compared to learning to excel at the game of golf?' asked the young chief executive, in some surprise.

'It's only a very rough analogy,' I replied. 'Yet golf and leadership have in common the fact that there are basic principles underlying both arts. The picture of white golf balls flying high and true onto the green and trickling down the hole reminds me of a better analogy for leadership.'

'What's that?'

'What do you think it is that makes flight possible?'

'Being an engineer by background I ought to know the answer to your question,' said the young chief executive with a smile. 'It is, of course, the Laws of Aerodynamics.' He paused while I waited, and then continued. 'You are not going to ask me what they are, are you? If so, I shall really have to dredge down deep into my memory of what we studied in applied mechanics at university.'

'It may be worth your while,' I said. 'For possibly there are equivalents to the Laws of Aerodynamics in the leadership field. If so, understanding them may enable you, as the chief pilot, to get the jumbo jet of a large organization airborne. Incidentally, *pilot* comes from the Greek word for a steering oar: the person qualified to steer the craft – the leader.'

'But everyone knows that leadership is an art, and by talking about possible equivalents to the Laws of Aerodynamics you are beginning to make it sound like a science,' protested the young chief executive. 'For a subject to be a science you do indeed need well-established laws or principles, together with theories tested by properly conducted experiments.

'When I was doing an MBA we had a module on Leadership,' he continued. 'I vaguely remember numerous so-called theories about leadership – Fiedler's Contingency Theory, Hersey and Blanchard's Situational Leadership, Blake's Grid, Emotional Intelligence, to name the ones I remember. "Leadership is the most studied subject in the world and the least understood", one lecturer quoted at us. We were told that none of these theories was proven or conclusive, just ideas. Some claimed to be based on empirical experiments, but the samples were so small and culture bound that it was impossible to take them seriously. As there was no agreement, the lecturer said that he would teach all the theories and let us make what we could of them.'

'How did you find that?'

'Extremely confusing.'

'So would I have done,' I said, 'but I think the confusion was needless. For over the past 50 years I think we have made real strides in establishing a knowledge base in leadership – what *ought* to be taught on, say, an MBA programme even if, owing to a shortfall in the knowledge of the staff, it isn't actually taught.

'The starting point is what I regard as the basic question in the leadership field:

> Why is it that one person emerges and is accepted as a leader in a group rather than anyone else?

'At least to my satisfaction,' I continued, 'it has now been clearly established that there are three broad ways of answering that core question. They can be compared to paths or approaches that snake their way up a mountain from different directions. The summit of the mountain – the pure essence of leadership – is, as it were, shrouded in mist. For leadership, like all other forms of personal relations, will always have about it a dimension of mystery.'

'What do you mean by leadership being mysterious? I hadn't thought about it that way before.'

'Simply that it contains elements that arouse one's wonder, stimulate one's curiosity, and baffle one's efforts to explain it.'

'Sounds rather like the Universe,' he said. 'But that's just a challenge to us to find and follow clues and to interpret evidence in order to find a satisfying explanation.'

'True, but you don't have to reinvent the wheel. We should be willing to stand on the shoulders of those who have studied the subject before us. The three paths I mentioned are well-trodden, clearly visible and from an aerial viewpoint you will see that they converge as they near the cloud-topped summit. In other words, they are complementary. The three signposts are:

- QUALITIES – what you *are*;
- SITUATIONAL – what you *know*;
- FUNCTIONAL – what you *do.*'

'That all rings bells,' said the young chief executive, 'I am sure I have come across those three approaches before. What is the latest thinking about them?'

Leadership Characteristics

'Let's take first the Qualities Approach – what you *are*. You may recall that when the first academic attempts were made to identify the necessary and desirable qualities of leadership it produced considerable confusion: lots of lists of leadership qualities were produced and there was apparently very little agreement between them. We have about 17,000 words in the English language to describe personality or character traits and so there is a considerable choice! Therefore those who were trying to study leadership on an empirical or "behavioural" science basis in America after the Second World War tended to dismiss the Qualities Approach as a busted flush on the grounds that no one had discovered the qualities that make a born leader.'

'Surely they were right?' interjected the young chief executive.

'Not really. The error they made was that they were looking for the appearance of the *same* word in the different lists, such as courage or initiative. What they should have done was to cluster words into *concepts*, or, if you like, sets of synonyms around a core idea. So that, for example, there is a set of words that revolve like satellites around the nucleus concept of a bold and determined attitude that is undaunted by difficulties and fearless in the face of danger: *backbone, courage, fortitude, grit, guts, resolution, spirit* or *tenacity.*'

The chief executive looked puzzled. 'But didn't I read somewhere that there are no synonyms in the English language?' he queried.

*I Cannot Hear What You Say
Because What You Are Thunders At Me*

'No *exact* synonyms,' I agreed, 'but nearly the same meaning in some or all senses. For words gather moss over time – overtones or nuances that cling to them. All the above words, for instance, when used loosely indicate the same core concept. Used more precisely, however, there is a distinction between, say, *courage* – the mental or moral strength to venture, persevere, and withstand danger, fear or difficulty – and *tenacity*. The latter has overtones of firm determination to achieve one's ends, with hints of stubborn persistence and unwillingness to admit defeat.

'In a similar way there is a distinction between *character* and *personality*, though both point to a bundle of traits, innate and learned, that distinguish one person from another. *Character* often points to an aggregate of moral qualities by which a person is judged apart from their intelligence, competence, temperament or special talents. *Personality* suggests more the whole indefinable impression received of a specific person.'

'To me *character* spells moral forcefulness, *personality* emotional appeal,' said the young chief executive. After some moments of reflection he continued: 'It's rather like colours. At home we are redecorating the kitchen at present and the paint catalogues offer an amazing range of different whites or yellows. It's as if *courage* and *tenacity* are two shades of yellow.'

'Not the greatest choice of colour!' I laughed.

'The next step I made was to distinguish between *typical* and *generic* leadership characteristics.'

The young chief executive asked me to explain the differences. I said that in my view leaders tend to exemplify or personify the qualities or attributes that are *typical* of the group to which they belong. For example, physical courage is a typical quality in the armed services, because all soldiers, sailors and airmen, whatever their rank, leaders or not, need a degree of physical courage. In other words, it's a military virtue. What effective military leaders do is to exemplify the key typical qualities expected in their milieu. And we can apply the same principle, I argued, to nurses, accountants, salesmen, doctors, academics, and so on. In every field of human endeavour you can specify – or its practitioners can – five or six key qualities required in a *good* nurse, teacher, engineer, etc. These 'local' qualities are what I call the *typical* ones, and together they form – or at least a 'critical mass' of them form – a necessary condition for leadership. It is easy to find them: all you have to do is get a few focus groups of wise professionals in any field to list them. You can grade the responses roughly into three categories according to the strength of agreement as follows:

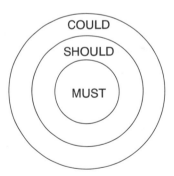

MUST – the essential attributes;

SHOULD – highly desirable ones;

COULD – characteristics that enhance but are not vital.

Nothing Great In This World Was
Achieved Without Enthusiasm

'But you are not saying, are you,' protested the young chief executive, 'that having the typical military qualities or virtues such as courage makes you a military leader, or that having the five or six characteristics of, say, a good research scientist makes you the leader of a laboratory? I play in an amateur orchestra and I can think of lots of musicians who have all the qualities of musicality, but they don't become conductors. It doesn't quite add up.'

'It's possible that you are confusing two ideas that should be kept distinct, namely *necessary* and *sufficient* conditions,' I replied. 'In science, these terms drawn from logic are useful for untangling intuitions about cause-and-effect relationships. For example, it is a *necessary* condition for certain chemical reactions that they take place in solution. But the fact of these chemicals being in solution does not guarantee that they *will* react with each other. Therefore, being in solution is not a *sufficient* condition that these chemicals will react. In general, as I understand it, scientists find it useful to agree on necessary conditions before they feel in a position to discuss sufficient conditions.'

'That sounds a most useful distinction and it's easy to grasp,' said the young chief executive.

The young chief executive glanced back through his notes and then continued: 'Using this tool, can we not now identify the necessary conditions that lead people to accept someone as a leader? I suggest that what you called the set of contextual or typical qualities forms one necessary condition. The potential followers have to see that the leader is *like* them in all important respects but *unlike* them – different or 'better' if you like – in other key respects. Moreover, I suggest that the more *generic* qualities of leadership belong here too. For a person is a whole. It would be artificial to divide their personality or character up into typical and generic qualities. Anyway, we have yet to identify these universal hallmarks of all good leaders – the generic ones I mean.'

'Why don't you help me to identify them? What would you place at the top of the list?'

Our discussions on the various contenders for universal leadership virtues ranged far and wide. Eventually, however, we homed in on the following characteristics:

- *Enthusiasm* – a state of extreme readiness and interest in some prospective action or subject, together with a willingness to be involved in it. It leads to activity undertaken with gusto, verve and exuberance.

- *Integrity* – moral soundness or excellence: the undeviating adherence to truth and a code of values. Integrity implies trustworthiness and incorruptibility to a degree that one is incapable of being false to a trust, responsibility or pledge. It's the quality that inspires trust in others.

- *Warmth* – a positive emotion, indicating sincere interest in or affection for others. It is allied to humanity – showing basic human attributes such as kindness and consideration.

- *Courage* – firmness of mind and spirit in the face of danger or extreme difficulty; the capacity to be a risk-taker.

- *Judgement* – the mental processes that lead to sound decision-making and problem-solving and estimates of people.

- *Tough but fair* – being without softness, especially to oneself, realistic and unsentimental; being strong or firm, but flexible; and being even-handed in all one's dealings with the team, ie not having favourites.

On Enthusiasm

The young chief executive and I agreed that this list of generic qualities was open-ended. How about *calmness*, or *high energy*, or *resilience*, or *humour*, or *compassion*? Each true leader revealed these and other qualities, like facets of a revolving diamond.

'So enthusiasm comes to the top of the list,' reflected the young chief executive. 'I have certainly never encountered anyone whom I would call a leader who lacked it, have you?'

'I cannot think of one,' I replied. 'Enthusiasm comes from the Greek verb that means *to be inspired*, literally *en* (within) and *theos* (god). The primitive idea, of course, was that exalted states of mind or passions were caused by the temporary or permanent possession of a person by some spirit or god. *Panic*, for example, comes from the Greek god Pan.'

'It's amazing what you can learn from words,' reflected the young chief executive. 'When you unpeel them like a chestnut you get to a shiny and often quite tangible core of meaning. Is passion the same as enthusiasm?'

'It's often used as a synonym, and in this context it means an object or feeling of desire or deep interest. I prefer enthusiasm

– a lively or eager interest in a cause or activity, plus an energetic and unflagging pursuit of it.'

'And it inspires enthusiasm in others too. It's contagious,' said the young chief executive.

'Yes, as a general principle *like inspires like*. For example, love inspires love, trust inspires trust. So if you want to inspire people for the work in hand, *be inspired about it yourself.*'

'That could hardly be more simple,' he said.

'In my National Service I served in the Arab Legion in Jordan as adjutant of a Bedouin regiment. One evening out in the desert, sitting and waiting for the brass coffee pots to sigh on the hot coals, a tribesman quoted a Bedouin proverb that has lived with me ever since: *What comes from your heart is greater than what comes from your hand only.* People will always respond to what they hear or see is in your heart.

'The effect of a change of leader – an enthusiastic one in place of one lacking any powers of inspiring others – can seem quite magical, even where the work in question is drudgery or toil,' I continued.

'Can you give me an example or two of this principle in action?' the young chief executive asked.

'Will you settle for a couple of examples from classical times? Xenophon, a Greek general who had in his early twenties explored in the company of the world's first and greatest teacher of the subject, Socrates, gives us two examples. The first comes from his observations of life aboard the Greek war galleys known as triremes, with three tiers of rowers drawn from the lowest class in Athens. Xenophon often sailed in the triremes, though he excelled as a commander of cavalry. To get the best out of these oarsmen – freemen not slaves – called for the kind of uplifting yet demanding leadership that produces enthusiastic teamwork, resulting in a great performance. Xenophon writes of the rowing-masters who could do it as if they were conductors of a winning chorus in the national competition:

On a warship, when the ship is on the high seas and the rowers must toil all day to reach port, some rowing-masters can say and do the right thing to sharpen the men's spirits and make them work with a will. Other rowing-masters are so lacking in intelligence that it takes them more than twice the time to finish the same voyage. Here they land bathed in sweat, with mutual congratulations, rowing-master and oarsmen. There they arrive with dry skin; they hate their master and he hates them.

'Xenophon achieved lasting military fame when, age 26, he became the leading general of a Greek mercenary force known as the Ten Thousand, who made an epic 800 mile march to freedom from the heart of the Persian empire when their employer was defeated and killed in battle. Xenophon proved to be an inspiring military leader himself, but he was equally renowned in the ancient world as a prolific author. He wrote the world's first books on leadership in the form of Socratic dialogues. In addition, while living on his estates in the shadow of Mount Olympus, Xenophon added another 'first' to his list, the world's first book on management – in those days it was, of course, management of large estates rather than of industrial or commercial organizations. The Greek title of the book is the same as our word *economy*, which literally means household management.

The interesting thing is that Xenophon saw little or no essential difference between leading soldiers in battle, so they were willing and enthusiastic about the work in hand, and leading civilian workers on an estate. In other words, for the first time in history he conceived of leadership as a transferable principle. What he saw clearly is that human nature is the same, be it encountered in an armed Greek warrior, a sweating, toiling oarsman, a farm worker in the fields or a man with the lowest social status of all, a slave:

It is no less necessary for a farmer to encourage his labourers often, than for a general to encourage his men. And slaves need the stimulus of good hopes no less, no even more than freemen, to make them eager and steadfast.'

*In my enthusiasm and intensity I will very often push people
to the limits of their capabilities – and that must entail a
certain degree of risk. The great thing is that the risk pays
off when that person suddenly finds something in themselves
they didn't know was there.*

Sir Georg Solti, orchestral conductor

'I haven't heard of Xenophon before,' said the young chief executive, 'but he certainly understood a thing or two about leadership. He must have been the first person in the world to have understood so clearly the importance of the combination of enthusiasm, bravery and skill in a military leader.'

'Yes, you are right. Xenophon had seen soldiers under such a leader, as he said "working cheerfully, each man and all together, when it is necessary to work. Just as love of work may spring up in the mind of an individual soldier here and there, *so a whole army under the influence of a good leader is inspired by love of work.*" Consequently for Xenophon this kind of enthusiastic leadership is quite simply "the greatest thing in any operation that makes any demand on the labour of men."'

'And how necessary it is today,' mused the young chief executive. 'I wonder why we have undervalued good leadership so much...'

'Probably because we thought it was something inborn, some gift that you either have or you don't have.'

'Some chief executives assume that they must have it by virtue of the fact that they have risen to the top.'

'An unwarranted assumption in all too many cases,' I commented. 'Socrates and Xenophon pioneered the belief that leadership could be developed. They even identified some of the principles of leadership development that still apply today. Yet they were aware that some people are more gifted with leadership ability than others, especially when it comes to inspiring others.'

The young chief executive paused to reflect, and then continued: 'I can now see very clearly why enthusiasm belongs to our first necessary condition – the qualities in a leader. In a TV documentary on the life of Rommel they quoted the reason Hitler gave for appointing Rommel to command the Afrika Korps in 1941. Hitler had said:

> I picked out Rommel because he knows how to inspire his troops. This is absolutely essential for the commander of a force that has to fight under particularly arduous climatic conditions like North Africa.'

'Rommel certainly proved to be an inspiring commander,' I continued. 'But this story illustrates that just having a leader of his calibre – a general with enthusiasm, boldness and skill – is not enough. To be able to inspire soldiers with confidence, love of work and desire for victory is of no avail if one is lacking the other necessary conditions for success, such as organization, weapons, ammunition, repair facilities and air superiority. Moreover, Winston Churchill found in General Montgomery a leader capable of inspiring the Eighth Army with new confidence in itself and a certainty that Rommel and the Afrika Korps were not invincible – they could and would be beaten. Enthusiasm is the base of the quickening, animating and inspiring power of a true leader.'

'But surely there is more to it than that?' said the young chief executive.

'There is indeed,' I replied. 'But do you think that enthusiasm is within your grasp?'

'Of that I have no doubt,' he replied. 'It's a mystery to me, but my enthusiasm is like a fountain within me.'

'Then you are not far from being an inspirational leader.'

Keypoints: Part 1

- There are three broad and converging approaches to the understanding of leadership: *Qualities* (what you *are*), *Situational* (what you *know*) and *Functional* (what you *do*). All are important and should blend together.

- A leader should exemplify the typical qualities or attributes of a good performer in their field. If, for example, you wish to lead a firm of lawyers, you should possess the five or six characteristics of a good lawyer.

- There are also more generic qualities associated with leadership, such as enthusiasm, integrity, moral courage, the combination of toughness and fairness, warmth, and humility. Both typical and generic qualities are a necessary condition for someone to be recognized as a leader, but not a sufficient condition.

- An enthusiastic person tends to inspire enthusiasm in others, so enthusiasm stands first on the list of generic leadership qualities. Enthusiasm is extremely common and it is within your grasp.

- At times we all need encouragement. 'There is a point with me,' wrote Gerard Manley Hopkins, 'in matters of any size when I must absolutely have encouragement as much as crops need rain: afterwards I am independent.'

'He Has A Look Upon His Face
That I Would Fain Call Master.'
'What Is That?'
'Authority'

Your Position Never Gives You The Right To Command. It Only
Imposes On You The Duty Of So Living Your Life That Others
May Receive Your Directions Without Being Humiliated

Part 2

The Authority of Knowing

The young chief executive sat silently for a minute or two as he studied his notes. 'Necessary conditions,' he said. 'So far we have explored the Qualities of Leadership and identified them as being necessary but not in themselves sufficient. Is that going to be true of the second path up the mountain that you mentioned – the Situational Approach?'

'In essence this approach answers our key question *"Why does one person become accepted as leader?"* by declaring that it is not so much on account of any inherent qualities of personality or character, but because of a person's appropriateness to the given situation. It is memorably expressed in a well-known play by J M Barrie called *The Admirable Crichton* (1902), where a polymath manservant emerges as the leader of a party that includes his employers in London, shipwrecked on a desert island. In other words, put a person in one situation and they will be accepted as leader; change the situation and they won't.'

'What made Crichton so admirable among the castaways?' the young chief executive asked.

'Doubtless some qualities such as being cool, calm and collected. But essentially it was because he revealed an encyclopaedic knowledge – he knew what to do when his employers were out of their depth and at a loss. So the critical factor here, as Socrates was the first to identify, is *knowledge.* There are basically three forms of authority in human affairs, in no order of importance:

- *positional* – when you hold a superior position in a social or organizational hierarchy and have authority within defined limits over what others do;

- *personality* – an inner subjective kind of authority that some individuals possess, which in modern times has been labelled *charisma;*

- *knowledge* – the authority that stems from technical or professional knowledge, possessed for example by a doctor or an engineer.

The last is best summed up in the saying: *Authority flows to the one who knows.'*

'Didn't you mention Socrates, in connection with Xenophon, as a teacher of leadership?' asked the young chief executive. 'Did he discover the Situational Approach?'

'Difficult to say, as he wrote no books. But two of his young disciples – Plato and Xenophon – did write books in the form of dialogues between Socrates and various individuals. How far these later-published dialogues represent actual remembered conversation is a matter for scholarly speculation, but we can be sure that Socrates was the first to teach the Situational Approach, for both Plato and Xenophon teach it and both use the same example of the ship's captain, who has authority over sailors because he has mastered the skill of navigation, so it must go back to the lips of Socrates.'

'It must have been quite a revolutionary idea in those days. I suppose he saw democracy as the mechanism that allowed citizens to elect to the various offices those whom they judged to be the best or most knowledgeable candidates?'

'Absolutely. The corollary is, of course, that you needed an intelligent and discerning electorate as well as well-qualified candidates. Hence the emphasis upon the need to educate for leadership, a philosophy to which one lasting memorial is Plato's *Republic*.

'Socrates' concept of the knowledge appropriate to a leader – at least through the lens of Xenophon's mind – is a wide one. It potentially includes, as we have seen, knowledge or understanding of human nature, and knowing how to encourage and enthuse or inspire others with a love of work. But the models Socrates had in mind were the artists and craftsmen of Athens, especially those known for their technical or professional mastery.'

'I can see the importance of the latter,' said the young chief executive. 'But it's clearly more a necessary condition than a sufficient one, for we all know people who have it in abundance and yet they are not accepted as leaders. It is necessary as a leader to have it, though we could debate how far it has to be specialist or generalist knowledge in the field. Would you agree?'

'Yes, indeed. The degree of technical or professional knowledge a leader needs depends on the field and their level of responsibility. It is not necessary, for example, for an orchestral conductor to have achieved excellence as a solo instrumentalist, though many have done so.'

'I am surprised you haven't told me the origin of the word *authority*,' smiled the young chief executive. He reached out and took another slice of gingerbread.

'A temporary reprieve! My own profession as an *author* is the clue. An author is someone who begins, begets, originates or creates something. It comes from the Latin verb *augere*, to grow or to increase. I like the idea that the Roman imperial title

Augustus originated from this verb and acquired other meanings later on, so that it was given to the leader who showed that he could grow the empire. But I wouldn't put money on that piece of etymology.'

'I can see the link with knowledge. An author or creator has a unique knowledge of the product, how it grew from the seed of an idea to the mature end-result. A conductor has authority, sure, but the true authority on a Mozart symphony must be Mozart. Likewise, a mother is always the chief authority on her child, or as far as any human being can be on another.'

'You can see, too, why an entrepreneur who builds up a large organization over years, growing it out of the seed of an idea, has a unique authority in that business. Of course that doesn't make him or her infallible, but that is another matter.'

'That's been useful,' said the young chief executive. 'Where next? I suppose we have now reached the third approach – Functional Leadership.'

Key Leadership Functions

The Functional Approach focuses, as you know, on the general theory that while all working groups and organizations are unique, each evolving its own distinctive *group personality*, yet all of them share in common *a set of three overlapping and interacting areas of need*:

- the need to achieve the common task;
- the need to be held together as a working unit (or team);
- the needs that individuals bring with them into the group, by virtue of being human beings.

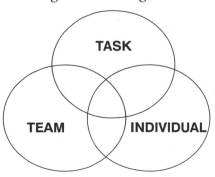

In order that the three areas of need should be met, or as it were satisfied, certain functions need to be performed. A function, as we have said, is roughly what you *do* as contrasted with what you *are* or what you *know*. In the context of a small working group, for example, here are the key functions:

- *Planning*
    - seeking all available relevant information;
    - defining the group task, goal or objective;
    - making a workable plan (in the right decision-making framework).

- *Initiating*
    - briefing group on aim/objectives and plan;
    - explaining *why* as well as *what, how, when, where* and *who*;
    - allocating subtasks and setting performance standards.

- *Controlling*
    - ensuring that all actions contribute to objectives;
    - influencing tempo;
    - maintaining group standards.

- *Supporting*
    - expressing acceptance of persons and their contributions;
    - developing the potential of individual team members;
    - encouraging group/individuals;
    - disciplining group/individuals;
    - creating team spirit;
    - relieving tension with humour;
    - reconciling disagreements or getting others to explore them.

- *Informing*
    - clarifying task and plan;
    - giving new information to the group, keeping them 'in the picture';
    - receiving information from the group;
    - summarizing discussion coherently.

■ *Evaluating*
- checking feasibility of an idea;
- testing the consequences of a proposed solution;
- evaluating team performance;
- helping group/individuals to evaluate own performance against standards.

Designated Leaders

'You say that these are necessary functions, not needed all together – every section of the orchestra playing at the same time – but as and when they are required. But I notice you did not say that they are *leadership* functions in that only the designated leader can perform them.'

'Some groups – jazz bands, string quartets – don't have a designated leader,' I replied. 'Theoretically any member can perform any function. I can think of a small company making pure fruit juices that is run by a triumvirate of its three young founders, who are the directors of finance, production and marketing, respectively – there is no chief executive. Early American theorists used to say that whoever contributed something that could be classified under one of these broad functions was the leader for the moment.'

'So groups no longer needed designated leaders?'

'Yes, that was their position, reinforced by what they perceived to be the failure of the traits theorists used to establish the existence of such a thing as leadership qualities. The talk was of leaderless groups being the thing of the future, the new democratic (good) model as opposed to the old authoritarian (bad) one associated with having a designated leader.'

'How did that work out in practice?'

'Not very well. In the "group laboratories" (as they were called) that gave rise to the new dogma, the groups studied had no real task to do, their mission being entirely one of group-introspection. Even there, however, there were leaders, though they were called "trainers" or "facilitators". Outside, in the real world, the doctrinaire abandonment of designated leaders proved to be counterproductive. A Russian symphony orchestra, for example, did away with its conductor and played sitting facing each other in order to try and keep together. They eventually decided to get another conductor. In Britain the National Health Service also experimented with the same dogma and experienced a similar disappointing result. More often than not, working groups do need a designated leader.'

'What about that small company you mentioned?'

'As they grow larger in size and the complexity increases, they will be compelled to select a leader, a "first among equals". It's the difference between being a string trio and becoming an orchestra.'

'How do people get selected as leaders?'

'Basically in two ways: you can be either elected or appointed. As a broad generalization, where groups throw up their own tasks they tend to elect their own leaders who are accountable to the electors. Trade unions and sports clubs are good examples of this practice. By contrast, where tasks are given to groups from on high, as it were, leaders tend to be appointed. Such leaders are primarily accountable to the authority that entrusted them with both the task and the group.'

'Quite a big difference,' commented the young chief executive.

'Ideally both elected and appointed leaders should be chosen from those who would have emerged naturally in that field or situation – the "admirable Crichtons" if you like.'

27

'And all three approaches – Qualities, Situational and Functional – would be needed to explain why one person rather than another *emerged* as the leader.'

'That's it. The British prime minister begins life as an *emergent* leader; he or she is then *elected* by their party and the voters; finally they are *appointed* by the Crown.'

'Does that mean that all the functions you listed are now to be regarded as the preserve of the designated leader?'

'He or she is accountable for them. Moreover, basic leadership training should develop the awareness and understanding needed to know when each is required, together with the skills to provide them. But any group of more than five people needs more functions than any one individual can supply. Therefore a wise leader will encourage others to share the work of meeting the task, team and individual needs.'

'How does that principle apply to decision-making? There is a strong belief still around that leaders should be the decision-takers. Isn't decisiveness a generic leadership quality?'

Sharing Decisions

'Decisive, yes, but that means the ability to take decisions at the right time and in the right way. A decision can be visualized as a cake that can be shared in different proportions between those concerned. The leader can have all the cake, make the decision and announce it. Or, at the other end of the spectrum, the leader can seek as much consensus as possible. Obviously factors like the time available and the relative knowledge or experience of the parties – leader and others – come into the equation. There is no one right point on the scale: the optimum solution depends on the appraisal (which should become instinctive in time) of contingent factors in the situation.'

'Are there no enduring principles, no "laws of aerodynamics", involved here?'

'One obvious principle is that in most exercises of judgement – the mental activity behind decision-making – as the proverb says, *Two heads are better than one*. When time is short even to the point of crisis a wise leader with skill may consult, listen and weigh the input of other people. Generally the consulting process, providing it is not done in a ritualistic, perfunctory or indifferent way, results in a better quality of decision. That is why, for example, companies have boards of directors or generals hold councils of war before taking big decisions.

'A second important principle is that *the more a person or group shares a decision that affects their working life, the more they are motivated to carry it out.* It's common sense really. If you are told to do something by someone in authority over you, you may do it. But if they want your heart and mind to be involved, if they want you to have a sense of responsibility, they will involve you in the decision as far as it is realistically feasible to do so.'

'You are doing no more here than stating the cornerstone of democracy,' observed the young chief executive. 'People will tend to obey laws that they or their elected representatives have had a hand in casting. "No taxation without representation." '

'By sharing leadership in this way, especially by consulting and listening before making decisions, a good leader helps to create the right context in which people can give their best. They feel free, respected and valued. In this climate the creativity that is so often latent within us can find expression. In a literary sense, *context* is those parts of a discourse that surround a word or passage and can throw light upon its meaning. The context I have just described doesn't directly inspire people – other factors are necessary for that – but it contributes to the right environment.'

'Just as the quality and nature of the soil – nutrients, earthworms, moisture – will engage the attention of the wise gardener who wants to win gold cups for his flowers or vegetables,' said the young chief executive. 'It's becoming clear to me that a lot of factors are needed to build a climate where inspiration becomes possible. I thought that it was just a question of standing up like King Henry V before Agincourt and giving people a rousing pep talk. It's more complicated than that. I am not there yet, but at least I feel that we are on the right track. Let me write down some keypoints.'

Keypoints: Part 2

■ The Situational Approach emphasizes the importance of knowledge in leadership. Yet there are people who have outstanding technical or professional proficiency, but who are not seen as leaders by those who work for them. At best it is another necessary condition.

■ Groups or organizations are always unique but they share the three overlapping areas of need: task, team and individual. There is a pattern of functions that together meet these needs: Planning, Initiating, Controlling, Supporting, Informing and Evaluating.

■ Although in principle anyone could provide one or more of these functions, most groups have designated leaders who are accountable for them. They may be either elected or appointed – or both.

■ Being decisive does not mean 'shooting from the hip' and invariably making snap decisions. It means taking decisions in the right way and at the right time.

■ The more that groups or individuals share decisions that affect their working life, the more motivated they are to carry them out. Factors such as time and levels of knowledge affect how far decisions can be shared, but a wise leader presses for as much involvement as possible.

The summits of the various kinds of business are, like the tops of mountains, much more alike than the parts below – the bare principles are much the same; it is only the rich variegated details of the lower strata that so contrast with one another. But it needs travelling to know that the summits are the same. Those who live on one mountain believe that their mountain is wholly unlike all others.

Walter Bagehot

Part 3

Levels of Leadership

'Leadership in all organizations, institutions or society as a whole exists on different levels,' I began suggesting. 'At the first level the leader is responsible for a small team of about 10 people – *team* leadership. The *operational* leader is responsible for a significant part of the whole, and has more than one team reporting either directly or indirectly to them. The *strategic* leader is in charge of the whole, be it a working organization or a political community. That familiar word *strategy* is in fact an amalgamation of two separate Greek words: *stratos* (large body of people) and *egy* (leader).'

'That's interesting, this idea of levels of leadership,' said the young chief executive. 'The corollary must be that it's no good just having a great leader at the strategic level if your organization is useless at the team and operational levels.'

'Exactly. Apart from having effective leaders in office at all levels, you also need excellent communication and good teamworking between them. It sounds simple, but it's a truth that evades many organizations today. As Clauswitz once said, '*In war what matters is doing simple things, but it is very difficult to do them*'.

'And in peace too,' added the young chief executive, with a sigh. 'And, knowing you, you would argue that all leaders need training for these roles, wouldn't you?' he asked.

'Of course, I take that to be a basic principle. We know how to train team leaders, but we still have a lot to learn about how to develop leadership at operational and, still more, at strategic leadership levels.'

'And does the Three-Circle Model apply only to training *team* leaders?' asked the young chief executive.

'By no means. In *Effective Strategic Leadership* (2002) I proposed that all groups and organizations are unique – each has a distinctive group personality or culture of its own – but all share in common the generic structure of the three overlapping areas of need.'

'That's clear, or at least it is to me. I suppose one becomes a strategic leader after being a team and operational leader…'

'That is what could be called the natural progression,' I agreed. 'And one doesn't cease to be a team and operational leader when one becomes a strategic leader. For instance, you have to create teamwork in the top group, which will include the senior operational leaders, so that it spreads out and infuses the whole organization.

'Moreover, strategic leadership includes overall accountability for the operation of the organization – delivering the right goods or services, whatever they may be, at the right time and at the right price. For, as the proverb says, *An acre of performance is worth a world of promise*. With the three meta-functions – Achieving the Task, Building the Team and Developing the Individual – in mind, then, there seem to me to be seven generic *functions* of strategic leadership:

- *Providing direction for the organization as a whole* – knowing where the organization is going; having a vision of what it ought to be like in, say, three to five years' time; understanding clearly its end – the larger purpose it serves.

- *Getting strategy and policy right* – strategy is the route to the longer-term destinations; it is concerned with what is important in the context of that longer-term state towards which the organization should be aiming. Strategy here encompasses both strategic thinking and strategic planning. Policies are general decisions that help others lower down to save time in decision-making.

- *Making it happen* – the operational or executive function of strategic leadership, which includes getting out of the office to inspect what is happening, monitoring progress and reviewing performance against agreed targets in the strategic plan.

- *Organizing and reorganizing as necessary* – ensuring that the relation of the whole to the parts of the organization is optimum for the task in hand.

- *Releasing the corporate spirit* – encouraging and enthusing people at every level and, where possible, releasing the latent spiritual energy in people. The symptom of success here is high morale at every level and in every branch.

- *Relating the organization to other organizations and to society as a whole* – finding allies or partners among other organizations, sometimes by mergers and takeovers, and creating a spirit of cooperative teamwork with them; promoting excellent relations between the organization and the local, regional, national and/or international communities.

- *Choosing today's and developing tomorrow's leaders* – choosing the best operational and team leaders is a critically important function. The strategic leader should also 'own' the strategic plan (evolved with the head of human resources and the top leadership team) for improving leadership capability throughout the organization. Have a passion for developing leaders!'

Practical Wisdom

After the young chief executive had considered the list carefully he asked: 'The role of strategic leader calls for a higher intellectual capability, doesn't it?'

Yes, but it's not exactly "brainy leadership" (as T E Lawrence once called it) that's needed. More what the ancient Greeks called *phronesis*, which was translated into Latin as *prudentia* and thus into English as *prudence*, a word that has acquired certain overtones not present in the Greek original. A better and more commonly used equivalent to *phronesis* is the phrase *practical wisdom*.

'Wisdom actually comes from the old Anglo-Saxon word for a *leader*, one who knows the way. Put at its simplest, wisdom is a blend of intelligence, experience and goodness. All those elements are required in one who is at the helm of an organization, especially in the turbulent seas of change. For, as the Roman poet Lucanus said, *"Anyone can hold the helm when the sea is calm"*.

'The Athenians held up several of their great leaders as exemplars of practical wisdom, notably Pericles, who led them in the long Peloponnesian War against Sparta, "like the helmsman of a ship who," writes Plutarch, "when a storm sweeps down upon it in the open sea, makes everything fast, takes in sail and relies on his own skill and takes no notice of the tears and entreaties of the seasick and terrified passengers."

'As for Thermistocles, he too had the power to reach the right conclusions when there wasn't much time for debate and he possessed foresight. He was particularly remarkable at looking into the future, Thucydides tells us, and seeing there the hidden possibilities for good or evil. To sum him up in a few words, it may be said that through force of natural genius and by rapidity of action this man was supreme at doing precisely the right thing at precisely the right moment.'

*Transcendent Common Sense Is The Rare Power
of Seeing Things As They Are Which Signifies Genius.
It Is The Ability To Draw Right Conclusions And To
Take Correct Action*

'I can understand why *intelligence* and *experience* are constituent elements, but why have you included *goodness*?' asked the young chief executive.

'Could we ever apply the term "wise" to someone who is not good? Greek philosophers in the school of Socrates saw conduct – personal or corporate – as a matter of choice. For them, choice necessarily involves not only intellect and thought but a certain moral state or character. It's the combination of the two that spelt *phronesis*, practical wisdom, which is why Aristotle numbers it among the four cardinal virtues, along with *justice, temperance* and *fortitude.*'

'But what's the connection with leadership?' he persisted. 'I can grasp *phronesis* as knowledge (intelligence and experience) applied to practical affairs, by which a person might know what to do or what not to do. I can see too that a quality of mind and temper is also implied: self-control, a lack of rashness as well as the ability to focus the mind on a problem before acting. Acumen, foresight, resourcefulness, circumspection, diligence in execution – being "on the ball" – yes, I can see that they are all necessary for right thinking and right action. I suppose you can break down what we call *decision-making* into three phrases:

■ *Deliberation* – courses open; probable and possible outcomes.

■ *Decision* – making the choice.

■ *Action* – acting on what is decided.

'In the deliberation phase I can see that a degree of *phronesis* is absolutely essential, and that a chief executive should be expected to possess it. But I still don't see where goodness comes into the equation. Integrity, yes, but *why goodness?*'

'Aristotle instances Pericles and others like him as demonstrating the nature of practical wisdom *because they can envisage what is good for themselves and for people in general.* He adds that this quality belongs to those who understand the management of estates – forerunners of our modern industries and businesses – as well as political states.'

'So if a leader is not a moral person, their vision of what constitutes the *good* of their state or organization will lack a moral component?'

'Yes, Socrates taught that all leaders needed a vision of leaving their organization or city in a *better* state than that in which they found it. He questioned Xenophon, for example, to establish that he had a clear idea as to how he could improve the Athenian cavalry – better horses, more training, improved leadership and so on. *Good* in this context is clearly a holistic term, as are its related words *better* and *excellent.* But alongside the technical and material elements there is also a moral ingredient. Admittedly the Greeks had two different words for *good* – *kalos* (technical, proficient skills) and *agathos* (morally good) – but they tended to see them as two sides of the same coin.'

'So *phronesis* is a moral virtue for the Greeks because it enables you to identify what is the true good for yourself and others. In modern organizational terms, it means – well, let me put it personally – if my aim is to see my company in a *better* state than it is now when I move on in, say, four or five years time, I need to have a holistic idea of what *better* means. Customer service, high standards of integrity and fair dealing, quality of products and services, finance and administration, the corporate spirit or morale of the company – all these may be ingredients of the vision.'

'Yes, so goodness isn't a separate entity: it's the wholeness of the whole, as invisible but as real as *health*.'

'You certainly know about health when you lose it,' reflected the young chief executive. 'I suppose that often it is only when a community or an organization loses its moral sense that it heads for disaster. By then it may be too late. The ship may be on the rocks and beginning to disintegrate.'

'True, and prevention is better than cure. The wise helmsman does not endanger his ship by ignoring the guiding moral stars in the firmament. It might be useful to think of three or four wise people you know. What are their characteristics?'

The young chief executive mentioned two or three names of people he considered wise, and began to talk about their characteristics. Old habits die hard and so I stood up and began to capture some of the qualities he mentioned on the flip charts, adding some more of my own as I, too, considered those whom I thought to be wise:

- exceptional understanding;
- seeing things from a larger perspective;
- understanding himself or herself;
- thinking for himself or herself;
- seeing the essence of a situation;
- grasping how various aspects of reality are related;
- sound, executable judgement;
- experience-based pragmatic knowledge;
- a clear idea of where the obstacles are;

- ability to assume contradictory points of view;
- width, height and depth;
- having a rich life experience;
- bringing clarity and form to experience;
- helping others in time of trouble;
- working with a person's natural focus of attention;
- being a good, sensitive counsellor;
- thoughtful, fair, not afraid to admit mistakes;
- acting within the limits of his or her knowledge;
- being comfortable with ambiguity;
- willing to profit and learn from experience;
- seeking the ultimate consequences of events;
- having moral and spiritual integrity;
- having an excellent character;
- searching for a way of life;
- reading between the lines;
- having an authoritative presence.

'Those 26 attributes – by no means exhaustive – of the people we consider to be wise in effect map the concept of *wisdom* or, more broadly, what we think a wise person *ought* to be. All I can add is to suggest tentatively that those attributes fall roughly into the categories that I have called *intelligence, experience* and *goodness*. It's always easier to remember three things than a long list.'

'It's more than just a memory aid, isn't it?' said the young chief executive. 'It's about trying to reduce complex things to their simple parts, teaching oneself to look for the essentials in a situation, the elements hidden under appearance. Isn't that necessary if I am going to be any good as a strategic thinker?'

'You are beginning to sound like a Greek philosopher,' I laughed. 'The concept of an *element* is a Greek discovery. Aristotle defined it as that which cannot be resolved into anything simpler, such as the irreducibly simple part of a compound or complex whole. The Greeks believed the physical universe was composed of only four elements: air, water, fire and earth. It took us about 2,500 years to establish that there are in fact more than 100 fundamental substances or elements to which matter can be resolved.'

'That begins to sound quite complex,' commented the young chief executive.

'It certainly does to me as a non-chemist, but in the late 19th century a brilliant chemist developed what we call the Periodic System. Classifying the elements according to their atomic weight, he was able to group them into four clusters or families. It's another good example of the power of the human mind to reduce complexity into a simpler form.'

Leaders and Managers

'Talking of scientists,' said the young chief executive, 'we borrowed their distinction between necessary and sufficient conditions. So if all the necessary conditions we have identified – contingent and generic *qualities*, professional *knowledge* and understanding of people, and *functional* 'three-circle' capabilities – are present in a person, will he or she be perceived as a leader? In other words, do the three approaches added together – the whole that is more than the sum of its parts – constitute the elusive sufficient condition we have been searching for?'

'We must be very close to it,' I replied. 'It has been said *that you can be appointed a manager, but you are not a leader until your appointment has been ratified in the hearts and minds of those involved.* It's when people start using the word *leader* about you that you, as it were, become a leader. That is why I always think of being called a leader as receiving an accolade, an indirect mark of acknowledgement.'

'I imagine that if people do not ratify your appointment in this way, you remain merely a *manager*. Is this how leaders differ from managers?'

'Perhaps a better way of putting it would be to say that it explains how managers who are leaders differ from those who are not. A *manager* in this context simply means someone who is responsible for managing a business or public service, or a part of one. It has replaced the much older job name of *administrator*. Your MBA – Master of Business *Administration* – is a relic of those days.'

'Can you be a good manager without being a leader?'

'Yes, I think you can be a good manager – but not one of the best. If we speak of someone as being a good administrator or manager that implies that they have the typical qualities or attributes we expect in a manager…'

'They are reliable, responsible, trustworthy, hard-working, thrifty with scarce resources, plan ahead, keep to agreed procedures or systems, are prompt in business, open-minded to change, knowledgeable in their specialities, meticulous over detail, cheerful, fair and courteous in their dealings with staff and colleagues, keep in control of things, are loyal to the organization, achieve their targets, are good time managers – I could go on,' offered the young chief executive.

'No need,' I said, 'for you have just sketched in roughly what makes a person a good manager. You will notice that the list doesn't contain some of the attributes we associate with leadership, such as providing direction, creating teamwork, leading by example and inspiring others. These are not alternatives: they are the extras, if you like, the added value, that leadership brings to management. If the managerial attributes are there, it is comparatively easy to move from merely being a good manager or supervisor to being on the path that leads to becoming a business leader at the level appropriate to the person – team, operational or strategic.'

'So you don't stop being a manager at a certain stage and become a leader?'

'Did you cease to be a son when you became a husband, or give up being a husband when you became a father? There is no such thing as a leader in the abstract. You will never walk down the street and see a leader. You will see a politician who is a leader, an accountant who is a leader, a doctor or nurse who is a leader, a teacher who is a leader, a military commander who is a leader, a police officer…'

'Alright, alright, I've got the message,' laughed the young chief executive. 'Well, I am glad that you reminded me that leadership is an abstraction, a kind of mental periodic table for arranging in clusters all the elements we see in leaders in various fields.'

'There is, however, a very useful broad distinction to be made between *managing* and *leading*, always bearing in mind that it is not either/or but both and…'

'A spectrum of some kind?'

'Precisely. And I think we can now identify fairly clearly the *situations* that call for something more at the *managing* end of the spectrum and those that activate the leadership cells towards the other pole. Any guesses?'

He Showed Himself Such An Example Of Kindly Wisdom,
Such A Combination Of Serious Purpose,
Humanity And Courtesy,
That The Others Had No Thought In Their Minds Save To Labour
With One Common Will For The Success Of All

The Challenge of Change

'That's fairly easy,' said the young chief executive, 'in a nutshell it is *change*. People with the typical managerial characteristics we have just identified could run an organization that doesn't have to face change. Of course now, with almost no exceptions, all organizations are having to respond to massive, continuing change. There's a much higher level of anxiety, people lose their sense of direction. In fact it's not unlike what happens when the flat surface of the sea *changes* to mountainous white-topped waves, the wind howls, darkness falls – then everyone senses the need for a good helmsman, that experienced leader that Plutarch talked about.'

'Having been a deckhand on an Arctic trawler in a great storm, when we battled against the black ice that was encrusting the superstructure and tilting us over, I can confirm what you say from first-hand experience,' I agreed. 'So the critical factor is change. Change throws up the need for leaders; leaders bring about change. *The bird carries the wings, but the wings carry the bird.*'

'What would happen if a leader tried to bring about change in an organization that was in a situation totally resistant to change, one that perceived no need to change?' asked the young chief executive.

'That's a theoretical question but an interesting one. My hypothesis would be that the organization would ignore him as an irrelevance, and if he persisted they would metaphorically crucify him. A rejected heart transplant might make a better metaphor these days. He would try to change things, but if there wasn't enough change in the environment it would be a fruitless task.'

'It's almost as if change is the fuel or power source of leadership,' mused the young chief executive.

'Certainly a true leader will never complain about change – for that is what makes leadership both necessary and possible. It's the *raison d'être*. If you go back to the original metaphors of a journey: all journeys are *changes* in location that take place over time. This morning you are here. By this evening you will be somewhere else. If you stay where you are, then time will elapse but no change of location will take place.'

'But there are journeys and journeys,' said the young chief executive. 'Going on a guided tour to Provence for your holiday is one thing, but exploring unknown territory is another. Guides can be hired for the first kind of journey, but leadership of a different order is required for an expedition into new, unfamiliar, unmapped territory. And the future begins to look more like that every day!'

'Most journeys, of course, are metaphorical. A school or hospital will tend to remain at the same location, but over time it may change from one state to another, it may become a worse institution or a better one – that's a journey too.'

'Becoming a worse institution suggests a lack of good leadership to me,' he said. 'Nowadays I don't think any organization can stand still. If it isn't getting better, it is almost certainly going to get worse. Doesn't it simply mean, however, that all managers need to be managers of change?'

'How do you manage change?'

'Don't you know? There are lots of business books written about it, and plenty of conferences or seminars. Some "gurus" have specialized in change management...' and here he broke off to mention their names and some of the most recent books on the subject. Then he asked me to share with him what I knew about managing change.

People Need Leaders

'My difficulty with the phrase *managing change* may sound a bit academic to you,' I began, 'but let me share it with you anyway. *Managing*, as you probably know, comes from the Latin word *manus*, a hand. The main branch of derivation comes from the Italian word for handling war horses – the fine mastery we now call dressage. (Another contributing source is the French word for a household, hence the work of running one.) So *controlling* actual or potentially unruly *things* – horses, ships, swords, pens and (in Jane Austen's novels) young children – is the main sense.'

'We have added another *thing* to that list,' said the young chief executive, 'namely funds, finance, money. Stocks and shares can be pretty unruly! And material resources – like machines or power.'

'And by extension it makes sense to talk about managing time too. For though time is invisible and mysterious, it is undoubtedly a precious resource, one that should be husbanded carefully. As the old English proverb says, *An inch of time is worth a yard of gold.*'

'I can see what you are getting at. Change is not a thing, not a commodity, not a resource. So, strictly speaking, it can't be *managed*.'

'That is the case. For the same reason we cannot manage love or manage religion or manage happiness.'

'Where does that leaves us?'

'It is simple. We agree that all change is a journey, physical or metaphorical. It may be a welcome journey or an unwelcome one. It may start out with a known destination in mind, and turn out to be an adventure...'

'Can you give me an example of what you mean?' interrupted the young chief executive.

'Take a well-known British company called Whitbread. When I worked for them as a consultant over 20 years ago they were one of the leading breweries. Beer was their only product and their "destination" was to increase market share. But the journey took an unexpected route. Whitbread stopped brewing beer years ago, and it has just sold its last 3,000 pubs to the private arm of Deutsche Bank for £1.6 billion. "Future" Whitbread will now consist of hotel, restaurant and leisure brands such as Beefeater, Pizza Hut and David Lloyd Leisure – at least until the next turn in the road.'

'It sounds to me as if they are making the road up as they go along.'

'Or reinventing themselves. One agent of change was strategic thinking. Here the key was to see their product and service in the context of the "bigger picture". Whitbread, historically (since the 18th century) a brewer and owner of pubs, began to see itself in a more conceptual or abstract way as belonging to the leisure industry. Thinking generically like that led them to see their essential business as leisure, not brewing beers, and opened up a whole set of new choices.'

'A new journey,' he said. 'But the top leadership still had to take their managers and workforce with them. With closures and redundancies it couldn't have been easy.'

'So managing change can only mean identifying new and positive directions, making a strategic plan, communicating truthfully and fully to all who must effect the changes – as well as be affected by them – and, above all, creating a positive and hopeful climate, one that makes people eager to embrace the challenging new opportunities ahead.'

'But isn't all this leadership?'

'If you are right – and I believe you are – "managing change" was just a piece of business-school jargon, a bolt-on to the concept of management in the years before the importance of leadership came to be recognized. *We manage things but people need to be led.'*

'Hold on,' cried the young chief executive. 'How about man-management or human resource management?'

'We should dismiss the term "man-management" as belonging to a vanished era. Field Marshal Lord Slim told me that it was introduced into military jargon not long after the Indian Army produced a training manual entitled *Mule Management*! Sometimes I have heard wives talking about *managing* their husbands – presumably unruly ones – but the word used in relation to people usually carries, as here, overtones of manipulation.'

'And managing human resources?'

'Not a phrase that stirs my heart. It can imply that people are *things* – resources – on a par with money or machines. It has now replaced *personnel*, a word from the French military vocabulary used in contrast to *materiel* – the material weapons, equipment and logistic elements of an army. We don't have a good name for what used to be called the personnel function, so "human resource management" survives *for want of better*. Perhaps later we can return to the phrase, however, as the inner meaning of "human resource" is worth exploring.'

The young chief executive mentioned that he was going to New York in a few days on business. While there he planned to attend a seminar on *Transformational Leadership*, a title that intrigued him. I said that I would look forward to sharing what he learned, and we concluded as usual by identifying some keypoints.

Keypoints: Part 3

- Leadership exists on different levels. A team leader is in charge of the primary group. An operational leader is responsible for a significant part of the organization. A strategic leader leads the whole and is, in Ovid's phrase 'a leader of leaders'.

- In order to discharge their seven generic functions, strategic leaders need to develop 'practical wisdom', a blend of goodness, intelligence and experience.

- Being a manager is not the same as being a leader. But to say that someone is a *good* manager implies that they have some leadership within them, just as being a *good* leader implies administrative ability.

- Some situations call for managers and others for business leaders (using business in the widest sense of where people are busy). The critical factor is change. Change throws up the need for leaders; leaders bring about change.

- Only things can be managed – money, business, affairs, machines. You cannot manage people – they can only be led.

We Awaken In Others The Same Attitude
Of Mind We Hold Towards Them

Part 4

Giving and Receiving

We began by discussing the three-day-seminar in New York. The young chief executive explained to me what had happened.

'The speaker outlined in his opening talk the difference between *transactional leadership* and *transformational leadership*. He referred to J MacGregor Burns as the author of this landmark in leadership theory, in his book *Leadership* (1978). You must have read it?'

'I have certainly glanced through it. It's a large book mainly about American political history, I seem to recall. I believe Burns was a professor at an American university in the field of politics or government. The phrase he actually used was *transforming leadership*. Later someone altered the phrase to *transformational leadership*, thereby subtly altering its meaning. Anyway, before we get onto that issue, what did the speaker have to say about *transactional leadership?*'

'Very little,' the young chief executive recollected, and checking through his notes he confirmed that had been the case. 'Beyond the brief reference to it in the opening talk we heard nothing more about it over the next three days.'

'Sounds rather as if it was no more than a straw man put up just in order to be quickly knocked down,' I commented. 'But the speaker must at least have told you what it was?'

'Yes he did. *Transactional leadership* merely implies that some exchange of value in order to get things done, arrived at by a bargaining process, has taken place. Beyond this transaction there is no sense of mutual commitment to a continuing higher purpose. To me it sounded more like a description of management rather than of leadership. What do you think?'

'It sounds as if the speaker was talking about a contractual relation where money is exchanged for labour. That entails a transaction – or a series of transactions – but it cannot be defined as leadership for it meets none of the necessary criteria we have been busy identifying. It appears to be a straightforward misuse of a term.'

'So should we dismiss it as worthless?'

'No, for most ideas have some value in them. It may be that the mistake was to *contrast* in a black-or-white, either/or way, the transactional element in human relations with the transforming or transformational element – whatever we discover this to be. In my view the transactional is the foundation on which the house rests. Did the speaker say anything about that?'

'No, he was silent on that subject.'

'Well, in that case it may be worth our while to explore this aspect of leadership for a moment. As I see it, *reciprocity* is a fairly fundamental principle in all human relations. To generalize, all human relations involve some form of give and take, a degree of mutual exchange. Reciprocity also implies the notion of an *equal* return or counteraction by each of two sides in relation to the other. If it's mutual, then the same thing is given and taken on both sides. Mutual respect is a good example. *A* has respect for *B*, and *B* in return has respect in equal measure for *A*.'

The young chief executive reflected about some of the relations he had experienced, and how in some of them the balance between giving and receiving changed over time, so one person was giving more and the other person conversely was receiving more than they gave.

'I notice you used the adjective *equal*, is that something we are born with or do we have to learn it?' he asked.

'Equivalence – the equal value of giving and taking – seems to be a guiding norm in human relations, which isn't to say that it's always the case. As you have just observed, few human relations have perfect symmetry in this respect; they may have it for a time, but time and change have a way of altering the balance. There is certainly a case for saying that our instinct for equivalent reciprocity is a matter of nature and nurture. I find it fascinating that in the first six months of a human baby's life its mother hands objects to it and it takes them. Gradually the baby is encouraged to hand them back. By the time the baby is about 12 months' old these exchanges involving giving and receiving have become more or less equal. The exchange of smiles probably follows the same pattern. Gorilla mothers and their babies do not follow this instinctive path.'

'This must be the basis for bartering – the exchange of one commodity for another,' observed the young chief executive.

We Cannot Live Only For Ourselves. A Thousand Fibres Connect
Us With Our Fellow Human Beings;
And Among These Fibres, As Sympathetic Threads, Our Actions
Run As Causes, And They Come Back To Us As Effects

The Importance of Being Fair

'Yes, and of course barter was eventually replaced – or largely so – by the introduction of money as the principal means of exchange. But barter or its monetary equivalent is merely the commercial expression of that underlying principle of reciprocity, a part of that much bigger web of interchange that links all of us as humans together. There is an expectation of giving and taking – usually in all human relations, and leadership is no exception,' I said.

'Are you suggesting that there is such a thing as transactional leadership?'

'Well, there is a transactional element in it. Often, where employment is concerned, it involves the exchange of money for time, skill and energy. I think it is vitally important that true leaders should be vigilant to ensure that the basic contract of exchange is honoured in a fair way – in the spirit as well as the letter of the contract. For example, people should get paid on time and receive all that is due to them. For satisfying that background, *impersonal* mutual obligation is a necessary condition for a fully personal relation.'

'Isn't that a matter of acting with integrity and fairness – qualities you mentioned in the beginning?', asked the young chief executive.

'Yes, but it's more a form of *justice* really – one of the cardinal virtues that the ancient Greeks and Romans expected in their leaders. The Roman lawyer Justinian expressed it in a nutshell: *Justice is the constant and unceasing will to give everyone their right or due.* A distinguished British Lord Chief Justice, Lord Denning, described justice as a spiritual thing with no satisfactory definition, though as a working definition he proposed that "*it was what right-thinking men and women believe to be fair*". Denning's use of the word "spiritual" reminds me of a saying that lingers in my mind: *Justice is love in impersonal relations.*'

'So in your view *transactional leadership* could be interpreted positively as honouring the spirit as well as the letter of the "contract" that exists between leader and followers. I hadn't realized that there is a spiritual aspect to it. Food for thought.'

'Notice, too, that there are two broad types of contracts: spoken or written contracts, and unspoken or unwritten contracts. The former are *explicit* agreements, sometimes exactly spelt out in all their details, so that there is no room for ambiguity or reason for difficulty in interpretation. Work for lawyers here! An *implicit* "contract" by contrast is left largely unexpressed.'

'So in an *implicit* contract how do the parties know what are the elements or "clauses" of the binding agreement if nothing is written down and no one talks about it?' asked the young chief executive.

'The extent – sometimes the existence – of these implicit "contracts" is revealed by situations that arise. As a general principle, the more impersonal the relation, the more we tend to make the contract explicit. The more personal the relation, the more we rely upon unspoken mutual understanding and trust.'

'Obviously explicit contracts are involved in all forms of employment – at least nowadays – but is there an underlying implicit contract in leadership? After all, the leader–follower relation can be an intensely personal one.'

The Implicit Contract

'Yes, I think there is an implicit or "psychological" contract underlying all leadership. Expressed in its simplest form it reads something like this:

> If you lead, we will come with you.
> or
> If you will accompany me, I will lead the way.

'As I say, this implicit understanding is seldom put into words; it is sensed and accepted by both parties. It usually develops over a period of time – it grows – and it invariably reflects a degree of mutual respect and even a deeper mutual feeling which may be called love,' I added.

'Soldiers who experience such respect and affection for their leader, for example, may prefer to die themselves rather than desert him in battle. For his part, the leader will sometimes lay down his life for his men. Anyway, by leading soldiers into battle from in front the leader is placing himself at greater risk than his men.'

'You are talking about loyalty, aren't you?' enquired the young chief executive. 'Such a leader creates loyalty so that people – in industry or on the battlefield – are loyal to him and would follow him anywhere. Surely this is the essence of good leadership?'

'Loyalty – personal loyalty of the kind you mention – is a double-edged sword. In other words, there is a downside as well as an upside. So perhaps we should pause for a moment to dissect the concept. Originally loyalty meant to be faithful in allegiance to one's lawful government. Later this meaning was extended to faithfulness to a private person, such as a leader – one to whom fidelity is held to be due. In that sense it would be possible, I suppose, to express the leadership "contract" I outlined as a kind of two-way or reciprocal loyalty.'

'You definitely don't sound too keen on the word loyalty,' said the young chief executive, with a smile.

'My difficulty partly lies with the notion of being a follower of a particular leader. Apart from the fact that being a follower sounds rather passive – like sheep following a shepherd – my objection is that it emphasizes too much devotion or loyalty to the *person* of the leader rather than the *cause* at stake. It gets really pernicious when the leader invites or persuades his "followers" to follow him in some path that is inimical to the cause.

'Please don't misunderstand me,' I continued, 'for I am not saying that it is wrong for a personal bond to develop between a leader and those who accompany him or her on the journey. As I have said, initial ignorance or even fear may turn into mutual respect and trust. That in turn is the breeding ground of mutual affection and may even develop into a love that is willing to make considerable sacrifices. That's the way we are. Yet both wise leadership (and wise "followership") rests on the principle that an implicit "contract" is not an unlimited liability on both sides. There are conditions, which may be implicit at first but frequently need to be made explicit as circumstances reveal them.'

Triangular Relations

The young chief executive and I discussed friendship and marriage as possible examples of personal relations that – at least in their higher forms – come close to having a character of 'unlimited liability'. Even with marriage or being a parent, however, we found that more often than not there was some limit, some unspoken condition, even if it never came into operation. The slogan *My country right or wrong* struck us both as an unsatisfactory statement.

'It's as if there is a hierarchy of loyalties,' he continued. 'A leader who orders his followers to commit a crime or something that is immoral should not be obeyed because a higher loyalty comes into play, namely a loyalty to what is good or true. It's a matter of values.'

'Yes, when someone gives you an order, there is a fraction of a second when your brain computes whether or not to obey it. Even the most strenuous attempts to "brainwash" humans so that they act under command like robots – efficient, insensitive, brutalized – can seldom totally eradicate the moral reflexes of the soul, at least where the brain of the person concerned is not vitiated by mental disease.'

'Then it is as if values are a third element, as it were distinct from the two parties. It reminds me of the idea that integrity means adhering to values outside oneself, especially truth. Isn't this a fundamental principle about human relations, that they are always triangular – there is always a reference point?'

'Whether or not it's a fundamental principle, it's true that it makes a difference whether you regard relations as essentially dual – consisting only of persons or parties relating to each other – when it is as if the two are looking together at, say, a landscape or a road ahead.

'The classic example of the dual relation must be the first stages of romantic love, when two lovers are absorbed by each other to the exclusion of anything or anyone else. Shakespeare is full of such pairs of lovesick lovers.'

'In real life, a few couples spin a cocoon of an *egoism à deux* for themselves. But most discover a third focus of interest...'

'The arrival of children does it, if nothing else,' interjected the young chief executive. 'A crying baby in the middle of the night is definitely "triangular" – I speak from recent experience! Your three-circle model – I notice you always put the TASK on the top – suggests that what each INDIVIDUAL (which includes the designated leader or leaders) and the TEAM triangulate on is the TASK. Therefore, by definition, it is *common*, or at least capable of becoming so.'

'Yes, but I am not arguing here that it necessarily feels common. It's just a fact. There is a job to be done that one person cannot do on their own. However the situation has been reached, it is a common task for this pair of individuals or group of people. Therefore all relations involving leadership are triangular. Talk about leaders and followers can obscure that fundamental fact.'

'Has that always been the case?'

'It probably goes back to our prehistoric past as hunter-gatherers, when men were companions in the endless chase. Evolution conditioned us to work together in pursuit of an elusive quarry. Writing in *The Four Loves* (1966), C S Lewis sees the origins of male companionship and friendship in "early communities where the cooperation of the males as hunters and fighters was no less necessary than the begetting and rearing of children. And to like doing what must be done is a character-istic that has survival value. We not only had to do the things, we had to talk about them. We had to plan the hunt and the battle. When they were over we had to hold a *post mortem* and draw conclusions for the future. We like this even better..." '

'In terms of the three-circles, then,' commented the young chief executive, 'the common TASK is the hunt, and the needs of INDIVIDUALS are met by sharing out the meat. As for the functions, Lewis has mentioned two already – *planning* and *reviewing*.'

'Yes, but he isn't looking at it through the lens of the three-circles model as such. What Lewis highlights is the "pleasure in co-operation, in talking shop, in the mutual respect and under-standing of men who daily see one another tested, that underlies the whole process".'

'Rather sexist, isn't he?'

'Well, he was a man of his time,' I replied. 'Lewis saw this necessary companionship of hunters in order to survive as the matrix of friendship. Here is what he has to say:

> Friendship arises out of mere Companionship when two or more companions discover that they have in common some insight or interest or even taste that the others do not share and which, till that moment, each believed to be his own unique treasure (or burden)...
>
> Companionship was between people who were doing something together – hunting, studying, painting or what you will. The Friends will still be looking together, but at some-thing inward, less widely shared and less easily defined; still hunters, but of some immaterial quarry; still collaborating, but in some work the world does not, or not yet take account of; still travelling companions, but on a different kind of journey. Hence we picture lovers face to face but Friends side by side; their eyes look ahead.

'I should add that Lewis does not undervalue companionship. "We do not disparage silver by distinguishing it from gold," he says.'

'Both companionship and friendship then are – in your phrase – triangular relations,' said the young chief executive. 'I suppose the corollary is that people who want to do nothing or who lack any interests can hardly find companions or friends. If you are not going anywhere, how can you find yourself among fellow-travellers?'

> *Life Has Taught Us That Love Does Not*
> *Consist In Gazing At Each Other*
> *But In Looking Outward Together*
> *In The Same Direction*

'That is what Lewis is suggesting. Notice his use of the *journey* motif, both in the literal and metaphorical senses. The shared journey or quest, if you like, is the third point of the triangle.'

'So it can be an actual journey, like the hunt, or a more abstract one like the search for a scientific truth…'

'Yes, all military operations are examples of actual journeys by land, sea or air – journeys made especially hazardous by being made into the face of an enemy. As you say, many other journeys we make are non-physical in nature, but nonetheless real. They involve colleagues and usually a leader – the first companion. Banesh Hoffman wrote of his experience as a colleague of Albert Einstein: *If you worked with him he made you aware of a common enemy – the problem. But you became his partner in battle.*'

'*Partner in battle,*' said the young chief executive, 'I like that phrase. Just to summarize where we are. There is a transactional dimension in all relations. Where it is explicit a leader should ensure that contracts are fairly, fully and honourably met. There is also an implicit or "psychological" contract, which has to be honoured in spirit, but it's not a blank cheque. A third force, such as values, may set limits or conditions on the leader–follower relation. In fact there is always a third element – in any leadership equation – namely the common TASK. Could you now help me to see where *transformational leadership* that I heard about in New York fits into this picture?'

What Transforms People

'We agreed, I believe, that there can be no such thing as *transactional leadership*, for merely honouring mutual agreements meets none of the necessary conditions we identified for explaining why the term *leader* can be used for anyone. Let's assume it's a way of talking about old-style management. So we are left not with a genuine choice between two alternative forms of leadership, but with only old-style management or *transformational leadership*. Have I got that right?'

'So far so good. The transformational leader is one who transforms or changes those working for him or her into high performers.'

'Did the speaker tell you how this transformation was to be achieved?'

'He used lots of buzz-words like vision, empowerment and charisma, and told some vivid stories of companies that had been transformed. I have hard copies of his PowerPoint slides here...' We looked through them, laughing at the cartoons, but we could find no very clear answers to how you changed people. It was mainly an exhortation to be charismatic.'

'Charisma may work in some situations, not in others. Could the speaker offer you any guidelines as to when his remedies would work and when they would not?'

'He was silent on that point.'

'Well, you should ask for your money back,' I said with a smile. 'It sounds as if *transformational leadership* assumes a dual model of relation, where A "transforms" or changes B so that B becomes a peak performer.'

'You mentioned that J McGregor Burns used a different form of the word – was it *transforming* leadership? What did he have in mind?'

'Burns' idea of transforming leadership was more interesting in that in his concept *both* followers and leaders are changed, and also the change is expressed as being for the better in a moral way. Followers are changed into leaders, and leaders become moral agents in enabling others to grow as persons.'

'It still sounds essentially a dual model,' said the young chief executive, 'but at least there is reciprocity: each is changing the other. Does Burns have much to say about how this positive interaction, leading to moral improvement and high levels of motivation, comes about?'

'Not much, I'm afraid. It happens, he says, when people engage with each other in a certain way. Burns tells us that the best modern example of a transforming leader is Gandhi, who, he says, aroused and elevated the hopes and demands of millions of Indians and whose life and personality, he believes, were enhanced in the process.'

'Yes, there is something noble about Gandhi,' mused the young chief executive. 'But surely it was a triangular relation? Gandhi gave spiritual leadership to the Indian people – the most spiritually minded on earth – on the long journey towards political freedom from British rule. He attempted to lead them, too, on the even more uphill road to social equality for all people in India, including the poorest and lowest castes. If you had put Gandhi in charge of car production at Ford and told him to transform the workers so that they had higher motivation levels and greater productivity, would he have succeeded?'

I laughed at the thought of a barefooted Gandhi in his white robes trying to transform the assembly-line workers in Detroit. Charisma isn't transferable. Nor is personal charisma enough. There has to be a set of factors or forces at work in a situation that creates the phenomenon that Burns was attempting to describe.

'That dimension of nobility – that factor that changes both leader and followers for the better – must be limited to your TASK circle,' said the young chief executive, who had also been thinking quietly to himself. 'If the common purpose isn't a noble one, then there is a vital dimension missing.

'Putting it another way, your three-circle model is incomplete,' he continued. 'Although it is perfectly legitimate to talk about the interrelation of the needs of *task, team* and *individual*, the model now should be extended to encompass the interactions between the values in the task or common purpose, the team or organization, and the individual person. My hunch is that it is some chain reaction of values in this triangle that leads to the phenomenon of transformation of character and transcendence of motivation. Perhaps we should take each of the three elements – the PURPOSE, the PEOPLE and the LEADER – in turn and explore how the values in them contribute to inspiration. What do you think?'

'It's worth exploring. But first let's write down the keypoints so far.'

Keypoints: Part 4

■ Reciprocity – the equivalence of giving and taking – is as fundamental a law in the sphere of human relations as the law of gravity is in physics.

■ Consequently, in all personal relations there is a transactional 'impersonal' basis. It is important that leaders honour these explicit or implicit contracts in letter and spirit. It creates and maintains trust.

■ There is a 'psychological contract' in leadership: *If you lead, we will follow; if you follow, I will lead.* Not everyone grasps that underlying implicit obligation. A French revolutionary leader one day sat in a café and exclaimed: 'There goes the mob... I am their leader – I must follow them.'

■ Human relations have a triangular dimension. In working relations the area designated by the TASK circle is what we have in common. It is as if we are not looking into each other's eyes but looking outwards in the same direction. A good leader sees others not as personal followers but as companies and partners on a common journey.

■ Needs is only one side of the coin, the other is values. The values inherent in the task, team and individual circles take us more fully into the realm of leadership.

The art of the conductor is to be able to communicate with the musicians and, beyond that, coax from them an inspiring performance. I've seen enough in this business to know that the difference between a good conductor and a great conductor is that the great conductor can make them perform as he wants and throw that inspiration over the audience...

I believe, particularly with great musicians that I'm able to collaborate with, that the sky should be the limit. And therefore as I am prepared to take the risks and shoot for the limit, then why shouldn't they follow?

Sir Georg Solti, orchestral conductor

Part 5

Beyond the Call of Duty

'Reflecting on our last discussion,' began the young chief executive, 'I wonder if inspirational leadership is not so much a property that someone has – a set of charismatic qualities – as the product of interactions between the three factors we mentioned: people, purpose and leader. You see, I am following the idea that all human relations are triangular in form – a triangle with dynamos at each angle.'

'May I try to express it slightly differently? There is a well-known phenomenon of people working far beyond "the call of duty", often with far greater enjoyment or satisfaction, and sometimes with at least feeling that they have grown in stature as a result of their engagement. We could call this *transcendent work*, for want of a better phrase.'

'By *transcendent*, then, you mean activity that exceeds usual limits in quality and quantity, not something that is incomprehensible and lies beyond ordinary human experience?'

'Precisely. We know, too, that transcendent work can occur in a field as if by magic. For "control groups" working under the same conditions do not exhibit it. Indeed, they may turn in performances that are well below "the call of duty". So the question arises: *what is the explanation for this phenomenon?'*

'The example you gave from Xenophon's writings – the two sets of Greek trireme rowers (p 14) – well illustrates the point you are making. Xenophon sees the difference as lying in the personalities of the rowing-masters. One is obviously an inspirational leader and the other is not.'

'Yes, but to develop our hypothesis, for the phenomenon of transcendent work to appear there have to be *three* necessary conditions present – people, purpose and leader – which together add up to the sufficient condition. It's like a rainbow: the interactions have to be just right. A rainbow is the product of light interacting with droplets of water suspended in the air. Get the angle right and – given our knowledge of the nature of light and the function of prisms – we can explain a rainbow. We can admire and see it in many forms, enjoy it when present, notice it fading and regret its passing. It cannot be touched, stored, measured or bought – still less *managed.* It's not an object, like water in a tap, that can be turned on and off at will.'

'In those respects it's rather like a lot of other things, such as joy or happiness,' mused the young chief executive, 'which are highly valued, enjoyed when present and as deeply missed when absent. They, too, are the outcome of interactions. You can't hang onto them, as they seem to come and go as if they had a mind of their own.'

He Who Binds To Himself A Joy
Doth The Winged Life Destroy
But He Who Kisses A Joy As It Flies
Lives In Eternity's Sunrise

On Human Nature

'Doubtless there are necessary conditions for joy or happiness if one searched them out, but when it comes to our particular rainbow – transcendent work – we at least have a head start in that we know we need to look at three factors. So shall we begin by exploring what all groups and all individuals have in common, namely human nature?'

'Globally? Surely the fact that people live in different cultures and have lived at different periods in history will alter the picture?'

'Yes, hence the distinctiveness and variety of mankind – none of us is the same. But let us assume for the moment that under-lying all these individual and social variations there is a common human nature, something we all share. What would you pick out as its salient feature?'

'Obviously we all have bodies and therefore a set of needs: for food and drink, for shelter, for safety and self-preservation, for health. We are all born, grow up – or the fortunate do – grow old and die. We have minds as well as bodies.'

'We share too a double nature as being both social beings – our tribal legacy – and yet individuals. The word *person* best expresses our dual citizenship, for we only become persons in relation to each other. The word derives from *persona*, the mask that Greek actors wore in a drama and hence the role or character they played. It came to be used in Roman law for those who were recognized in the courts as having legal entity and thus being the subject of rights and duties. So we all have *personality* – the quality or state of being a person.

'That must – or I should say ought – to transcend the differences of race, colour, gender, disability, wealth and age,' I continued. 'All individual human beings are persons and, however much they act to forfeit their birthright by doing despicable or evil things, they remain entitled to be treated with respect as they have the dignity of being persons.'

'That is the case, though it is sometimes terribly hard for the parents of a child murdered by a violent paedophile to abide by this principle when their feelings or emotions are taking them in the opposite direction,' said the young chief executive. 'Human emotions can be so immensely strong. I suppose human nature is a compound of body, mind and heart, physical needs or instincts, reason and emotions. The speaker in New York told us, I remember now, that management is about the mind, while leadership deals with the emotions.'

Spirit Within

'I hope you are sceptical about that statement. At best it is a half-truth. For emotions are often confused with spirit.'

'So you would make a distinction between the two?'

'In this context, yes. It gives us a four-fold description of human nature as PHYSICAL, MENTAL, EMOTIONAL and SPIRITUAL. We are like aircraft that fly on four engines.'

'So you see them as sources of power or energy?'

'Physical energy is obvious, isn't it? Mental power is also something we talk about. Emotion and motivation are close – the *mot* in each of the two words comes from the same Latin verb "to move". It is not so clear that there is such a thing as spiritual energy, as my aircraft analogy posits, but maybe there is.'

'Sounds more like windpower to me,' smiled the young chief executive, shaking his sceptical head.

'You may not be far off the mark. *Spirit* comes from the Latin word for air or breath. As dead people do not breathe, the primitive mind supposed that life was in the breath. So in *Genesis*, for example, God breathes into man (*Adam* is the Hebrew word for *man*), whose shape he previously shaped from the clay, and man comes alive. God literally inspires or inspirits him, with life.'

'Like the kiss of life,' reflected the young chief executive.

'Of course the creation myth at the beginning of *Genesis*, with this anthropomorphic picture of God making man, is not to be taken literally. The concept of spirit as we know it took shape over centuries, as it acquired meanings or overtones above the original notion that it was life in the vital or biological sense. The following five developed senses of the word give us an idea of the present scope or range of the word:

- the active or essential power operating in persons;
- a particular character, disposition or temper which exists in or pervades or animates a person or a group of persons;
- the disposition, feeling or frame of mind with which something is considered, viewed or done;
- a person, group or organization considered in relation to its character or disposition;
- the essential nature or qualities of someone or some group, which constitutes its pervading or tempering principle.'

'There is quite a strong sense that *spirit* is the active or essential power of the inner self,' commented the young chief executive. 'In that respect how does *spirit* differ from *soul*?'

No Man Really Knows About Other Human Beings. The Best He Can Do Is To Suppose That They Are Like Himself

'Both refer to the indefinable immaterial essence, the animating or activating principle of an individual person. So neither can be located by the senses. That doesn't mean to say that they are not real, of course, for there are lots of things (like electricity) that we cannot see yet we know to be real. The word *soul* is used more when we think of something akin to the essential person, with functions, responsibilities, aspects or a destiny, or when its connection with the body is in view. Perhaps the nearest we can get to it is when we sense a more or less unchanging inner self within us – that which constitutes *me*.'

'And *spirit*?'

'That sometimes stresses an opposition or antagonism to the material or corporeal, as for example when we speak of spiritual values in contrast to material values. But it is the preferred word when the stress is on the quality, movement or activity of that essence or entity. *Soul* sounds a bit static, but *spirit* is always dynamic.'

'Yes, it's a much more dynamic word,' agreed the young chief executive. 'If someone is described as *spirited*, it suggests to me a person with a high degree of energy and vitality, mixed with a touch of daring. But it can also suggest an extraordinary buoyancy or resilience, a calmness or other worldliness, a refusal to go under or to give up. Maybe spirit is the energy of the soul,' he added, after some moments of reflection.

'To use again that earlier distinction, spirit is implicit, it is innate in us. Usually it is only circumstances that reveal its presence and nature.'

'There is another possible characteristic of spirit that is relevant here: the idea that it is something common, something we share – that it is not, as it were, private property.'

'Rather like the air we breathe.'

'And therefore it is possible – if that assumption is right – to communicate: to make common to all what one presently possesses.'

'Transactions of the spirit,' murmured the young chief executive. 'It reminds me of our discussion about reciprocity, especially where a mutual relation springs up where trust or respect is given and the same is received back in return.'

'Yes, I think those are examples of the wider communication I have in mind. If someone trusts another and that evokes a response in kind, could we not say that he or she had *inspired* trust?'

The young chief executive accepted that it would be normal to use the word in that context. It was a neutral term, he observed, since one can inspire mistrust, lack of respect, fear or hatred in others.

'It's very hard to separate the things of the spirit from the emotional and mental domains, isn't it?' he said. 'Some people can inspire emotions in others, such as love and fear. Others can arouse mental energies in others, such as interest and curiosity.'

'Impossible, for we are wholes and not sums of parts. Body, heart, mind and spirit appear to us to be an indivisible unity, though many hope that ultimately the soul survives. What is especially important in this context is that spirit is associated with the human capability for *transcendence*, for surpassing usual limits or the high-tide watermarkers of past experience.'

I Am A Little World Made Cunningly of Elements,
And An Angelic Sprite

To Solve A Problem Which Has Long Resisted The Skill And
Persistence Of Others Is An Irresistible Magnet In Every Sphere
Of Human Activity. There Is No Height, No Depths,
That The Spirit Of Man Guided By A Higher Spirit Cannot Attain

The Uses of Spirit

'You said a few moments ago that the word *spirit* is used when movement or activity is implied. Could it be that the spirit in us is naturally drawn to journeys – journeys of significance?'

'What an interesting thought!' I replied. 'I wonder if you might be right. Maybe even challenging physical journeys have some deeper resonance in our essential being. Have you noticed that all the world's fairy stories involve journeys set within the context of the eternal struggle between good and evil?

'Maybe it depends upon the journey, but some can become epics of the human spirit. Captain Scott's journey to the South Pole ended in failure and disaster, yet when we read his last letters we sense that other inner journey of the indomitable human spirit.

'One of the most experienced and best qualified of all the American astronauts, Storey Musgrave, was asked what motivated them to make the great journey into space not once but many times, in spite of the attendant dangers. "Depends on who you are," he replied, "but for me its 99.9% spiritually driven – a direct revelation of the cosmos, God if you will." Not since the 1960s, he added, have we had a vision that space travel is about people, what it means to be a human being.'

'That begins to suggest to me,' said the young chief executive, 'that there is indeed a *spiritual energy* implicit in us, a potential source of high-octane fuel. Given the oxygen of inspiration and a lighted match it can burst into life and generate new energy. Let me pause and write down a few keypoints.'

Keypoints: Part 5

■ Sometimes work is done in such a way that amazes observers in terms of its quality – it far exceeds what people thought they could do. Forces present in the task, in the people themselves, and the leader, interact to produce this result.

■ Human beings are like four-engined aircraft. The engines are body, mind, heart and spirit.

■ Spirit is difficult to define, but it relates to the essence of an individual person – what traditionally is called the soul. Spirit is dynamic rather than static. It suggests movement, energy and resilience.

■ In some way we don't understand spirit is also a common property. We have it but we also share it. It is that which makes possible the phenomenon of inspiration.

■ It leaves us open, too, to the idea that there is a higher power or spirit that may also inspire us in creative ways, guide us and strengthen us. Our sense of being on an inner journey is a fruit of our spiritual nature.

A Vision Without A Task Is A Dream
A Task Without A Vision Is Mere Drudgery

Part 6

The Common Task

'People, then, are spiritual human beings. Because we have a spirit we are capable of being inspired. We look for meaning and purpose. Our spirit is active or dynamic, so change, forward movement and journeys attract us at a deep level. What I suggest we explore next is the kind of task that is capable of evoking our full range of energies.'

'That surely must be a matter of values,' said the young chief executive. 'But before we come to that may I ask why the top circle – the apex of the triangular relation – is labelled TASK and not, more fashionably, MISSION or VISION. Quite frankly, TASK has an old-fashioned ring about it.'

'You may be right, but it's a question of choosing the right word, the one that must work at all three levels of leadership – team, operational and strategic. So it is general, and it implies little more than something that needs to be done. There's an element of *must* about it, an obligation of some kind – imposed from outside or within – to complete it. It is a psychological sense or feeling in groups, the *lust to finish* as John Wesley once called it. That is why it is appropriate to call it a group need.'

'The strength of that internal group need to achieve the task must vary quite considerably,' observed the young chief executive. 'Doesn't that take us immediately to the value the group attaches to accomplishing the task?'

'What do you think are the factors that come into play here?'

'To state the obvious, if the group itself or its individual members are to receive large financial pay increases or bonuses, then they will be more eager to achieve the task.'

'Yes, but these rewards are extrinsic – they are distinctly outside the task in question and are not derived from its essential nature. To complete the picture, we would have to sketch in the more negative penalties of not accomplishing the common task. For fear is a strong motivator. Soldiers, for example, who do not win a battle are liable to be killed in the rout or to spend a long period in captivity.'

'True,' he said, 'but these positive and negative consequences – the traditional sticks and carrots – are by their very nature completely unlike the given task. What are the intrinsic elements in a task – those that belong to its essential nature – that excite the enthusiasm and commitment of people, that make it potentially inspiring?'

'What does your experience suggest?' I asked.

The young chief executive considered the question and then suggested we look at actual cases. So we then discussed what constitutes the TASK circle in a wide range of organizations – those like his own producing goods or services for profit, government departments, public services like health or the police, schools and universities, sporting bodies, voluntary bodies, charities and churches. He mentioned, too, some of the tasks that he had found inspiring. Then he offered a tentative conclusion.

'The common element in the tasks that inspire – or are capable of inspiring – people seems to be that they contribute directly or indirectly to some wider purpose for good.'

'What is your concept of *good* in this context?' I asked.

'It could be social good – producing the goods and services that society needs – or doing good for needy or unfortunate individuals, as charities do. Public services are also, as the name implies, serving the good of the public...'

Service to Others

'There is an important distinction there,' I said. 'If I can use a personal example, after school my generation had to do two years of military conscription which in Britain was called *National Service* (originally a wartime phrase coined by Winston Churchill for civilians enlisted in the armed forces and applied by him to the post-war compulsory period). I experienced a strong sense of lack of purpose or meaning in those days filled with drill, cleaning equipment, training exercises, guard duties. History reveals, moreover, that my months guarding the Canal Zone, apparently to protect Britain's oil supplies, was a complete waste of time. I was not making anything, nor was I meeting the needs of individuals who needed help, like my girlfriend at the time who worked as a nurse for the Save The Children Fund in Jordan's refugee camps. Deeper reflection on Churchill's phrase, however, led me to see that one can serve a *nation* or a *society*, not just a needy individual neighbour. Moreover, in Milton's words: *They also serve who only stand and wait*. In the context of the Cold War and the circumstances of the day – including the levels of knowledge then available – my unchosen profession as a soldier had dignity.'

The young chief executive had been listening intently. 'One difficulty in the discovery you made while doing National Service goes back to the issue of reciprocity. If the Samaritan whom we call "The Good Samaritan" (the word good doesn't actually appear in the story) helps the mugged guy out of the ditch and gets him back on his feet, at least he gets thanked. There is a face-to-face, two-way personal relation of giving and receiving...'

'As Shakespeare wrote: *Thanksgiving – the exchequer of the poor.*'

'Yes, but my point is that society or the nation cannot reciprocate in that way. If you drive a train of commuters into London every day, you may be meeting one of society's needs, but there is no reciprocity from the passengers. It becomes a monetary transaction – you drive the train in return for your wages, while passengers pay the company to be transported in safety and on time from A to B. There is no personal relation, no personal reciprocity, to speak of.'

'That has to be the case. But, in my analogy of the soldier, the intrinsic fundamental of *service* is still there, though it is a more impersonal service to the *commonwealth*, not the personal service to an individual we normally associate with the word. Some soldiers do their work solely for wages – we call them mercenaries – but others are inspired by ideals such as serving the good of their nation or the international community, and prove themselves willing to sacrifice their lives in those causes. Train drivers are no different: a few are mercenaries, but most want to have a sense of making a valued contribution to the needs of society.'

'One of the fundamentals that underlies the larger design of the TASK, then, is an inherent value of *good*,' said the young chief executive. 'When that sense of higher purpose is lost or absent is when cynicism, apathy or hostility takes over. Mind you, that implicit quality of *good* may take some teasing out. But if it is not innately there, imprinted within the DNA of the TASK, we are left only with extrinsic goods.'

'And they are not to be underestimated. To reuse C S Lewis's metaphor, we should not think less of silver because it is not gold. If there is a necessity for *toil* – that is, work without mental, emotional or spiritual value – then rewarding or compensating the labourers with extrinsic *goods* such as money or other material rewards, together with appreciation for undertaking what no one else would voluntarily choose to do, makes their labour palatable and even satisfying. But unless they can see a purpose in it, some *good* the task necessarily serves, it will be as soul-deadening as turning an endless treadmill in a 19th century prison. For that is the way we are made.'

'Is *good* the only value that we should look for?' the young chief executive enquired.

The Value You Add Comes From
The Values You Hold

Three Great Values

'The value of *truth* seems to be equally important. You may recall that when we talked about *integrity* as a leadership quality that makes people trust you, the importance of truth as conceived to be something outside oneself, something to which one owned a primary allegiance, emerged,' I replied.

'In what sense can a task have *truth*? Let us assume that a leader, or anyone else for that matter, should in principle always tell the truth about the task in hand. Is that what you mean?' asked the young chief executive.

'Not entirely, though actually seeing clearly the truth about the task – the realities of the situation – is significant and we might return to that later. No, what I had in mind were those tasks that can be interpreted self-evidently or indirectly as pursuits of *truth*. All forms of education – for truth is the mind's good – and research in the sciences or arts fall under that banner. (Not, of course, the so-called academic research that is self-serving, banal and lacking a sense of exploration.) Therefore they tend to seem self-evidently meaningful or purposeful to us.'

'So, to take our present conversation as an example, it feels meaningful because we seek the truth about leadership?'

'Yes, and even if we got nowhere, the attempt, the journey, would I suspect seem worthwhile to both of us. The same can be said, I suggest, for tasks that involve or have the value of *beauty* implicit in them. A world-famous film producer said recently: "All my life I have a compulsion to make beautiful things. Beauty is for me an ideal that pulls me towards it." Her words capture the artistic or creative impulse that is encoded in our spiritual DNA, though some obviously have it in greater measure than others.'

'*Good, truth, beauty* – are there any other values that we should look for?'

'There is a broad tradition, emanating from the ancient Greek philosophers who were the first to explore this area, that these three are the chief values. Other values are satellite moons circling around these planets.

'It's interesting that the values appear to have some relation to each other,' I continued. 'Scientists and mathematicians, for example, often comment on the beauty of the truths they discover. The relation between truth and goodness is self-evident. Apart from implying someone who adheres to truth, "goodness" also (literally) means wholeness. It is hard to conceive of a person of integrity or a whole person who is not also good.'

'What of the relation of beauty and goodness?'

'Here again we tend to link them, at least subjectively. Beauty is the only visible value of the three, and we tend to assume that a beautiful person is morally good...'

'And an ugly one bad.'

'In a more sophisticated frame of mind we distinguish between an inner beauty as compared to an exterior or merely physical form of beauty. We all know that a lovely smile can transform a plain face, or that technically good looks can lack beauty. The inner kind of beauty seems to be the obverse side of goodness. As Shakespeare wrote in *The Two Gentlemen of Verona*:

Is she kind as she is fair?
For beauty lives with kindness.'

While I spoke the young chief executive had been doodling on some paper. He had drawn another three-overlapping-circles model, which he showed me.

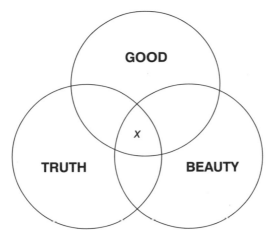

'I am curious to know what we might call x, the place where all the three values come together. If these ideals have their own drawing power; then the x energy must have a three-fold intensity.'

'We can only speculate about that,' I replied. 'If you reverse the image and imagine a task that is on the full overlay of evil, a lie and ugly – the Nazi extermination camps come to mind – the effects on humans, directly or indirectly, are appalling, almost too painful even to contemplate.

'I am not suggesting that goodness, truth and beauty are there in their pure forms, but we need at least a trace of them – a few drops of the supernatural in the bath of reality – to make our endeavours seem worthwhile, meaningful or purposeful.'

'Does x have a name?'

'No, it does not. Maybe *love* is a contender. For love is an energy or force, and it is the only thing we know that integrates the concepts of good, truth and beauty.'

Men think there are circumstances when they may treat their fellow beings without love, but no such circumstances exist. Inanimate objects may be dealt with/without love, but human beings cannot be treated without love. If you feel no love for people, leave them alone. Occupy yourself with things, with your own self, with anything you please, but not with people.

Leo Tolstoy

A Sense of Purpose

'What is the relation between TASK in your diagram and PURPOSE?' asked the young chief executive.

'As I mentioned *task* is just a general word signifying something that needs to be done. It does, however, usually suggest a limited, particular or non-recurring piece of work, or a circumscribed or short-term undertaking, whether voluntary or not.'

'And one that will require a relative amount of effort.'

'Yes, even to the point of being hard and unpleasant. What gives tasks their meaning or value is their *purpose*, or desired end result.'

'In that case, how does *purpose* differ from the other words that we commonly use for the result towards which someone or some organization chooses to direct activity, such as *aim*, *end*, *goal*, *object* or *objective*?'

'*Purpose* differs from them in two respects. First, it may suggest either a resolute, deliberate movement towards a result – being filled with a sense of purpose – or the desired result itself. It's energy plus direction. Secondly, and importantly in the context of our present discussion, the specific overtone of purpose in either use is that of *significance* – a key word that encompasses both meaning and importance. An *objective* (or one of the other terms) can be specified, quantified and measured – it answers the *what* question. *Purpose* is not amenable to measurement and answers the *why* question.'

'And purpose refers to those underlying values of good present in some tasks or kinds of work. I can see now why meaning and purpose are so often associated together – they are almost synonymous. Where does *vision* fit into this framework?'

> *It Is Provided In The Essence Of Things*
> *That From Any Fruition Of Success,*
> *No Matter What,*
> *Shall Come Forth Something*
> *To Make A Greater Struggle Necessary*

On Vision

'Vision is a much overused word nowadays, and I tend to avoid it if I can. Even pedestrian goals or objectives – sometimes merely ambitious intentions – are pretentiously presented as visions. Having said that, there is in fact quite a strong link between *leadership* and *vision*. Not surprising really, because leading in front on the way ahead implies that you can see – literal vision – the path. Hence the proverb Jesus quoted: *If the blind leads the blind, both will fall into the ditch.*

'Vision in the literal sense of the proper functioning of the eyes extends quite readily to the metaphorical idea of sharpness and understanding. In this sense it can indicate discernment or foresight – being able to "see over the horizon". You may remember that Thermistocles was credited with above-average success in inferring or guessing what the future might be, rather than imagining an outcome in accord with either what is hoped or what is feared. In relatively recent times Winston Churchill showed similar acumen in foreseeing the inevitability of war with Hitler and, later, that Communism would replace Fascism as the post-war enemy to freedom. Ordinary reasoning and experience, elements of *practical wisdom*, are enough to explain how Thermistocles came to his conclusions about the threat of the Persian Empire or how

Churchill reached his not dissimilar ones about the over-reaching imperial ambition of Adolf Hitler.'

'But isn't there much more to vision than a power to see what is not evident to the average mind or having above-average fore-sight as to what the future will be like?' asked the young chief executive.

'So far what I have said roughly falls within Jonathan Swift's definition: *Vision is the art of seeing things invisible*. To see what the world will actually be like in, say, 2025, to select the true scenario from many possible ones, is a form of "seeing things invisible", at least to others.'

'A scenario is an outline or synopsis of a play,' said the young chief executive. 'Doesn't that metaphor assume that the play is already written, and we are trying to predict what the scenes in Act 3 'The Future' will be, going on our knowledge of Act 1 'The Past' and Act 2 'The Present'? Perhaps we are the authors, not the audience, so isn't it us who write the script for the next scene?'

'Part-authors maybe, if you believe – as I do – in what Shakespeare called *a divinity that shapes our ends rough-hew them how we will*. There is some predictability in history, or, to put it slightly differently, some guesses are better than others. The study of history is valuable because it enables us to get to know a lot of people in their Act 2, looking forwards to their Act 3, and we are able to check their powers of foresight or their attempts to create new scenes. Such a study develops a sense of how the river of history flows. We can see some individuals who had a vision in the creative sense.'

'Like an artist's vision?'

'Yes, we are talking here not about the power of sight, literal or metaphorical, but about the act or power of imagination. And a vision here applies to what is seen. It may be something seen in a dream or hallucination, it may be illusory, imaginary, ideal or a supernatural appearance that conveys a revelation.'

'I can see why to call some plan *visionary* is a polite way of saying it's totally impractical and lacks any capability of realization!' laughed the young chief executive.

'What then constitutes a true vision?' I asked.

'It must be a blend of imagination – for you are envisioning a state or product that doesn't exist, no one has actually seen it – with realism. I mean it has to be feasible, given the resources available and the limits imposed by the "river of history". Henry Ford's concept of a car that every American family could afford, or the idea of man walking on the moon are examples of what you called true vision. Stretching, but possible. Also made real by the ability of the leader to work back to the present, thereby creating a path to the future.

'Bringing things down to earth,' concluded the young chief executive, 'it's the imaginative power to see growth possibilities for the future hidden in the present. *The seeds of the future lie in the present.*

Vision Is Seeing The Potential Purpose Hidden In The Chaos Of The Moment, But Which Could Bring To Birth New Possibilities For A Person, A Company Or A Nation

Vision Is Seeing What Life Could Be Like While Dealing With Life As It Is

Vision Deals With Those Deeper Human Intangibles That Alone Give Ultimate Purpose To Life

In The End, Vision Must Always Deal With Life's Qualities, Not With Its Quantities

---

Vision Is The Blazing Campfire Around Which People Will Gather. It Provides Light, Energy, Warmth, And Unity

'A true vision, then, defines the presently unseen result the team or organization is aiming for – that which informs the journey. It transforms change into a way of reaching a desired end.'

'Yes, the result is seen in "the eye of the imagination". Faith may be defined as believing in the reality of things unseen.'

'In all but literal physical journeys or voyages, don't all leaders require a degree of vision? How else can they provide direction on the journey?'

'What you say must be true. But, given the amount of contingency that multiplies dramatically beyond the relative probabilities of tomorrow – "chaos theory" – a flexibility over actual destinations is essential. In other words, when it comes to the future no one has 20:20 vision. As the proverb says, *In the country of the blind the one-eyed man is king*. It's moving in the right direction that matters.'

'With purpose?'

'There are visions and visions. But for visions to be inspiring, to serve a purpose and to elicit a sense of purpose – the spiritual energy that is released – they have to be touched with the red, blue and green of the *good, truth* and *beauty*.'

'Why those colours?'

'Because light refracts into those three primary colours.'

'It sounds to me as if you are elevating PURPOSE above VISION.'

'If we are talking about inspiration, yes I am. Hitler had a vision of a Europe without Jews, and the task he gave to his henchmen was to exterminate them in death-camps. It was a vision with no purpose or meaning, devoid of the cardinal values, therefore it could never inspire the spirit deep within us. I discount those temporarily taken in by Hitler's delusions.'

'To summarize,' said the young chief executive, 'we can discard TASK as being essentially time-limited. What matters is having PURPOSE, in the sense of having both a clear vision of the overall result or end of one's endeavours and that spirit or feeling of *movement* towards the desired result, however it is defined, being as it were drawn towards it like a magnet. That covers vision except in the special sense where an act of the imagination is involved, where something is to be first imagined, then shared with others and then created or made real.'

'If the vision has values of the kind we have been discussing, we call it a *creative* vision. The importance of the process you outlined is that it's the only way that the valuable *new* things happen in our human odyssey which, like pearls, we string together as *progress*.

'But don't chuck out TASK. For PURPOSE or VISION have to be broken down into *tasks* however we label them. Otherwise they remain merely an intention or a dream. Unlike purpose or vision, *task* spells effort, exertion, even struggle. A task can be hard, unpleasant, arduous, demanding.'

'But if it was easy,' he said, 'I don't think people would respond. Don't we find a degree of challenge in the very difficulty of such a task?'

The Need for Challenge

'But are they not put off if the task is impossible?' I counter-questioned.

'Of course. So there is a fine balance between what is far from easy and what is just plain impossible. Man can get to the moon on a space rocket but we cannot land on the sun.'

'That would certainly be an all-consuming experience,' I said, smiling at the thought. 'So a potentially inspiring task is one that offers to stretch you, to extend you in one or more dimensions of your ability, perhaps even your being. As Robert Browning put it:

Ah, but a man's reach should exceed his grasp,
Or what's a heaven for?'

'Isn't that how we grow?' interjected the young chief executive.

Possibly, if we stay stretched, as it were, and do not shrink back into our normal former or habitual selves like snails contracting back into their green-yellow shells. To be stretched is to be exercised beyond one's ordinary or normal limits. Arguably we all have some *stretch* – the capacity to be stretched – within us. Perhaps it relates to the spirit within us.'

'It doesn't really matter what we call it, I know what you mean,' said the young chief executive. 'Personally, I love a challenge.'

'A challenge is really just a summons of some kind, a metaphorical form of someone suddenly thrusting a legal writ or demand into your hands, or a sentry challenging a stranger to identify himself or herself, or being called to fight a duel to answer some affront. The variety of challenges we are more likely to face share their characteristics of being often threatening, provocative, stimulating or inciting.'

'Did you say inciting or exciting,' queried the young chief executive.

'It may be both,' I answered. 'Either way a challenge is a call to make a special effort, often at a real personal cost.'

Example Is Not The Main Thing In Influencing Others –
It Is The Only Thing

Moral Authority

'To challenge someone – to make a demand as if of right – implies the exercise of authority of an unusual kind,' mused the young chief executive. 'If the demand came from a leader, then he or she must have that kind of authority. He or she must be able to ask people not to spare themselves in such a way that they cannot say no.'

'How does a leader acquire such *moral authority*?' I queried.

'In the first instance they have to be able to show – if called to do so – that they have not spared themselves. They have to be able to uncover their scars. Leaders like Mahatma Gandhi and Nelson Mandela, who both endured suffering and imprisonment, have a certain nobility of character. Didn't their people sense in them what you just called moral authority? It is frequently lacking, alas, in those who rely merely on the authority of their position.

'Gandhi and Mandela had acquired the right to demand what they have already given.

'By the same warrant, no Board of Directors can call for sacrifices from their managers and workforce if they, as the senior executives, have taken up residence in Easy Street,' added the young chief executive.

'Or Luxury Square. Of course the Chairman of the Board can appeal for everyone to tighten their belts and work harder, using all the now familiar rhetoric of leadership – vision, inspiration, challenge, all the old familiar buzzwords – but *his words will lack power.*'

'That reminds me of the Zulu proverb about people not hearing what you say because of the thunder of what you are.'

'Yes, it is as if human nature obeys certain laws, and if we understand those laws it helps us to work with the grain of human nature rather than against it. We do not respond to leaders who do not share our hardships and dangers. Think back to that tragic day September 11, 2001 when terrorists destroyed the World Trade Center in New York. One name went round the world as a byword of leadership – Mayor Rudolph Giuliani. Why? Because he shared the dangers and suffering of his people.'

'Yet the leader is surely only voicing the challenge: it is there, implicitly or explicitly, in the situation.'

'That must be so, for there are plenty of challenges in life that come to us without any intermediary.'

'Like the challenge facing my son when he had to learn to walk again after a serious motorbike accident, or the target my daughter set herself to do a sponsored walk in the highest region of the Andes to raise money for our local children's hospice. Both these challenges involved elements of uncertainty and risk – they might not have made it.'

'If there was no such risk,' I replied, 'we might not interpret it as a challenge at all. If the outcome is absolutely safe and certain, it may not fully engage us.'

Keypoints: Part 6

■ TASK is a general word that signifies no more than something that needs to be done. We have to look behind it to see what PURPOSE the task is serving, for it's purpose that gives it value – the meaning that our spirit seeks.

■ The purposes that most inspire are those that are intrinsically good; they are often so because they contribute to the common good. Such service takes many forms, but there is a broad distinction between service that meets individual needs – with personal response as its bonus – and service that meets social needs.

■ The value of good is not the only source of inspiration. Truth and beauty – the other members of the trinity of great values – are also forces that draw us to seek them. Where the three overlapping circles intersect may represent the power of love as a spiritual force.

■ Purpose suggests both movement towards a result and the result itself. Of all our words for results – vision, ends, goals, aims, objects, objectives – it alone conveys the idea of significance, of values that confer meaning.

■ Vision is an act of creative imagination – the ability to see what no one else has seen or imagined possible.

■ Apart from having purpose, a task will not stir us unless it stretches us. As the Italian proverb says, 'By demanding the impossible we obtain the possible'.

Success as a conductor has nothing to do with movement. It has everything to do with the persona, the personality and a person's ability to communicate with the musicians and convey your ideas. The strength of the performance comes in conveying your involvement in the process, rather than being a god who wields the whip with the capacity to open and close the door. You must be someone who embraces and helps the orchestra. The most effective leadership, to me, is the leadership that doesn't look like leadership. The moment somebody walks in looking and sounding like a 'leader', that's quite suspicious to me. You must be part of the process – so convinced by what you are doing that everyone else has no choice but to follow you. It's intuition and personality. You have to encourage people to open up, seduce them, not scare them, to follow you. That's a great leader!

Paavo Järvi, orchestral conductor

Trust Men And They Will Be True To You

Treat Them Gently And They Will Show Themselves To Be Great

Part 7

Pulling the Threads Together

'Perhaps we can begin with a summary of where we are,' began the young chief executive. 'First we identified the key question: *why is it that one person is accepted as a leader rather than another?* The three "paths up the mountain" to answering the question were the:

- QUALITIES Approach – the contingent and generic characteristics of the person concerned. What you *are*.
- SITUATIONAL Approach – the emphasis here being possessing technical or professional knowledge appropriate to the situation. What you *know*.
- FUNCTIONAL Approach – the Three-Circles model of needs present in working groups and the key functional responses. What you *do*.

We explored, too, the idea that although most groups and organizations have designated leaders – elected or appointed or both – wise leaders do not attempt to perform all the necessary functions themselves: they share the work (if not the burden) of leadership rather than keeping it all to themselves. By involving others as much as possible in decision-making, for example, they generate a sense of responsibility as well as commitment.

'Then we had a discussion about necessary and sufficient conditions. I think you were saying that if a person scores high in all three approaches it is highly probable – nothing is certain in this life – that he or she will be perceived to be a leader and, where one is needed, accepted as such.

'Then the principle emerged that *leadership exists on different levels,*' he continued, 'and we identified three: the *team* leader (a direct descendent of the hunting party leader), the *operational* leader, who has more than one team reporting to him and heads up a significant part of the whole, and the *strategic* leader, who heads up the whole organization.

'Then we touched on the much-debated differences between *managing* and *leading.* You suggested that the simplest way of resolving the issue was to consider the kinds of situations that call for one rather than the other. Where there is little or no change, where things are governed by rules, where the organization can be conceived as a machine or self-perpetuating system, then it is appropriate to put it in the charge of managers who will plan, control, supervise and administer it on behalf of the owners, be they private, shareholders or the public via the instrument of government. Characteristically they achieve conformity and performance by the fear of people losing their jobs and by the provision of incentives such as monetary rewards or promotional prospects.'

The Parable of Flight

'By contrast, leaders are called for where change is dominant, where the climate is dynamic rather than static. Change can always be expressed in the metaphorical language of a *journey*. You are where you are now; you do not know where you will be tomorrow, but you know it will not be here – if you stand still or tread water you will drown. Leaders are those who know the way ahead. They can formulate a desired destination and identify the route that has to be taken, the steps along the way. More than that, they can inspire others to face and overcome the rigours of the journey. What is it about these leaders that makes them inspirational?'

'May I suggest a parable? You recollect that I used the analogy of the Laws of Aerodynamics to advance the thesis that there are certain timeless and timely laws or principles in the leadership field? If we explore the parallel further, it turns into a parable. Let me explain what I mean.

'Our modern concept of the Laws of Aerodynamics goes back to an English engineer, inventor and designer named Frederick Lanchester, who built the first experimental motor car in Britain, in 1895. Turning his attention to aeronautics, he laid the theoretical foundations of aircraft design in his book *Aerial Flight* (1908). Most of the Laws of Aerodynamics he identified in it stem from Newton's Laws of Motion. To them must be added an application of the work of Swiss mathematician Daniel Bernouilli, who pioneered the modern field of hydro-dynamics, the one touching on the conservation of energy: the flow of air over the upper wing is constrained by the shape of the wing – it accelerates over the upper surface, therefore pressure goes down and creates a suction on top of the wing. We must add, too, the Law of Continuity of Flow.

'Yet, amazingly, an acute Frenchman noticed that if one simply totalled up these laws, flight seemed impossible! Hence D'Abernet's Paradox, wherein he proved that on the basis of known laws flight is impossible, yet at the same time we know that flight is possible – birds do it.

'The solution to the puzzle lies in an assumption that has to be made about the nature of air. Namely, if you assume that air has low viscosity or adhesiveness, so that it sticks to the wings, then flight becomes intelligible. So among the Laws of Aerodynamics we find, of all things, an assumption. The parable is this: true leaders tend to make the assumption that people do have the seeds of greatness in them.'

'What do you mean by greatness in this context?' asked the young chief executive.

'I wouldn't like to try to specify or quantify it, but I am thinking again of magnanimity: that degree of spirit that enables one to bear trouble calmly, to disdain meanness and revenge, and to make sacrifices for worthy ends. The generous and courageous spirit, I submit, is not the quality of a few great individuals, but is spread far and wide in humanity. Those who exemplify it are the true nobles among us. Our word *noble* comes from the Latin verb for "to come to know". As we come to know people, either directly or through books, we sometimes discover that they are noble, that they do have outstanding qualities which situations – often great adversities – bring to the surface. And some of the noblest among us are children.'

The Task Of Leadership Is Not To
Put Greatness Into Humanity
But To Elicit It
For The Greatness Is Already There

Inner Greatness

'I hasten to add that I regard this as an assumption, no more. You cannot prove it.'

'But surely it can be falsified. Just think of all the people who display anything but greatness. If we began to catalogue all the forms of the littleness of human nature we should be here for aeons,' commented the young chief executive.

'Yes, it's a form of D'Abernet's Paradox again. We are both great and little. It's a strange mixture. Sometimes the greatness struggles against the other side, our littleness. It's an assumption – and act of faith – to believe that the greatness is foremost. Without it necessarily being a piece of conscious philosophy, leaders worth the name do believe in people – they trust them, have faith in them – and it is this belief that is the first step to drawing out the hidden greatness in people.

'The people really barred at the door of leadership are those misanthropists who hold a low opinion of people in general. A cynic, for example, is contemptuously distrustful of human nature and motives, and would sneer at any suggestion that such things as sincerity or nobility exist.'

'When I took over as a factory manager – my first job as an operational leader – I was pretty sceptical about people,' said the young chief executive. 'My policy to others was quite simple: prove to me that you are reliable and trustworthy, then I shall trust you. It was my experiences with Steve Down that changed me.'

'Can you tell me about that?' I asked.

'Just before I came into the job my predecessor briefed me about "the Problem", as he called it. The "Problem" proved to be one Steve Down, a 44-year-old manager who was the classic under-performer and a gloom-merchant as well. Nothing and nobody was ever right for him. "Down by name, Down by nature", colleagues said of him.

'Initially, and probably understandably, I was seduced into this paradigm of Steve. For that first few months I would climb all over his back, making sure that he worked the hours that I thought he should work and gave the effort I and the organization thought he should give. Then, having reflected upon the reasons why these attempts at influencing him were failing, I decided as an experiment to change the way I viewed him. It was like taking off one pair of glasses and putting on another that were rose tinted.'

'What effect did it have?'

'To begin with there was no change. The lesson for me then was to learn to be patient – not my strongpoint. The change in Steve over the next year, however, not only astounded me but amazed all his colleagues – even his wife, as I heard much later. At 44 he seemed to suddenly discover his life and became incredibly ambitious and hugely positive. When I first took over he announced to me that he never wanted to leave Liverpool, where our plant was. Then one day he came to me saying that he and his wife had decided to pursue a career in our Training Department, which was based in Windsor. You can imaging the satisfaction I enjoyed.

'It taught me that the key foundation stone for all good leaders is to have an enormous belief in their people. Furthermore, I believe that this can be taught. And once this foundation stone is in place, it is possible to teach every other aspect of effective leadership. So the world can produce the leaders it needs – we do not have to rely on an uncertain supply of "born leaders", and anyway there will never be enough of them.'

'I am surprised to hear you say that this *foundation* stone of enormous belief in people can be taught. I make a distinction between the knowledge that we are taught or learn on the one hand, and the knowledge we acquire. For example, we acquire our mother language. What I think happens is that we catch a glimpse of this greatness or nobility of spirit first in *one* person, and it alters our view of all other people for we have sensed an underlying pattern and are programmed to look for it. Just for fun, see if you can see a picture in these shapes:

Source: Open University

'Don't worry if you cannot do so – nine out of ten people can't. Here is the answer.' With that I handed to the young chief executive the solution (see p. 141). 'The point is this. Whenever you now look at the above collection of shapes – try as you may to prevent it – you will *always* see the solution-picture. If you don't believe me, try it out. And if you act towards people as if that solution picture is within them, they may well reciprocate by showing greatness. Isn't that what you learnt from Steve Down?'

Treat People As If They Were What They Ought To Be
And You May Help Them To Become
What They Are Capable Of Being

The young chief executive was silent for two or three minutes. 'Doesn't it stand leadership on its head?' he asked.

'If people are great, then they deserve to have great leaders. Up to now I have assumed that it was the leader that makes the people great.'

'You are nearer to the mark. What you said reminds me of what the Roman historian Livy wrote at one point in his history: *Rome being great deserved great leaders.'*

'So I have not discovered a new theory of leadership,' he laughed.

'If we jump a few centuries, we find Dr Samuel Johnson of dictionary fame commenting on what he called the *plebian magnanimity* of the English soldier. (The *plebs* were the common people of Rome.)'

'I suppose he meant by that what you said earlier about facing danger calmly and proving always willing to make sacrifices to worthy ends.'

'Yes, and the other military virtues too. Among them I would number cheerfulness and a sense of humour. Humour keeps things in proportion and lowers the tensions of the moment – it oils the wheels of daily living. But on occasion it can also express something we value in the human spirit. I like the saying: *Humour is an affirmation of dignity, a declaration of a man's superiority to all that befalls him.'*

'Did Johnson have anything to say about leadership?'

'Indeed Johnson did. The British redcoats, he said, expect their officers to lead them into battle from the front. For their part, he continued, the officers are confident that if they do so, the men will follow…'

'That's a perfect expression of the implicit mutual "contract" we were talking about earlier,' interjected the young chief executive.

'Johnson said that this occurs not because British soldiers lack bravery or initiative, almost implying that they could conduct themselves perfectly well without officers. Yet they accept such leaders as I have outlined as "a tribute to their own loyalty and *esprit de corps*". A tribute is a gift or service showing respect, gratitude or affection. Leadership as a tribute to those whom one respects and trusts – that reminds me of the great motto of Sandhurst: *Serve to Lead.*

'Johnson added that in the case of other European nations (before the French Revolution changed things) the officers do not lead their men into the fight but follow behind to ensure that no one skulks off to the rear when the first shots are fired.

'It's worth adding,' I continued, 'that one who leads soldiers into battle from the front is far more likely to get killed than anyone in the rank and file. For it's a natural instinct for soldiers to pick off the leader of the opposing forces, if they can identify them. They know that his death can cause panic, so that men break and run. Jesus quoted a proverb to that effect: *Smite the shepherd and the sheep will scatter.*

The Effects of Trust

'But surely great soldiers would stand their ground or continue to advance, with or without leaders?'

'All great soldiers are potential leaders if the call comes to them to lead. If the whole regiment is reduced to two privates, one will lead the other.'

'Such an army must be almost invincible.'

'No, it will lose battles from time to time, even campaigns and wars, for an enemy's sheer weight of numbers and *materiel*, together with superior generalship, can overcome it, but no defeat will be attributed to any shortcomings in team leadership, morale or *esprit de corps*.'

'If you trust people – I mean if you assume they are great like Johnson's redcoats – don't you run the risk that you will be let down?'

'It is highly probable that on occasion you will be let down. Therefore as a leader you need to work out a clear policy. What is the issue? For me it is encapsulated in a remark made to me by a headmaster: *If you trust boys, you will be let down; but if you do not trust them, they will do you down.*'

The young chief executive laughed. 'I know what he means,' he said. 'In my case it has been a matter of moving from an implicit policy of not trusting people until they have proved trustworthy to an explicit policy – I make it clear to everyone – of treating people as worthy of my full trust until they show themselves to be unreliable.'

'And have you been shown to be wrong often?'

'No, once or twice only. In one case it was really my fault because I put the person concerned in a position where she was out of her depth and I ignored family difficulties she was trying to cope with. The other person is someone in my senior team at present who just hasn't responded – yet anyway – and we may have to part company.'

'Does that lead you to alter your policy?'

'Not at all, for I reason why should I abandon the 96 or 97 people in every hundred who *are* great for the sake of the two or three who fail to live up to the promise within them. So far we have talked about individuals,' said the young chief executive, 'but does the same principle apply to organizations?'

'I believe it does. As you know, every organization develops its unique group personality, its culture and its prevailing climate. Often, but not always, this is shaped by the founder's legacy of a set of enduring values – "the way we do things here". Hence Emerson's principle: *An institution is the lengthened shadow of one person.*'

> *I Prefer To Have Too Much Confidence,*
> *And Thereby Be Deceived,*
> *Than To Be Always Mistrustful.*
> *For In The First Case,*
> *I Suffer For A Moment At Being Deceived,*
> *And, In The Second, I Suffer Constantly*

'Where that ethos rests on that key foundation you identified – an enormous belief in people – it can have an almost tangible presence. You may have come across Charles Dickens' description in *David Copperfield* of the school where David was so happy:

> It was very gravely and decorously ordered, and on a sound system, with an appeal, in everything, to the honour and good faith of the boys, and an avowed intention to rely on their possession of those qualities unless they proved themselves unworthy of it, which worked wonders. We all felt that we had a part in the management of the place, and in sustaining its character and dignity. Hence, we soon became warmly attached to it.

'That would fit any good school today,' I added.

'Or business company,' said the young chief executive. 'Haven't we identified a fourth path of understanding up that mountain of leadership which you said was cloud-topped in mystery?' With that he wrote on the flip chart:

What you ARE – Qualities
What you KNOW – Situational
What you DO – Functional
What you BELIEVE – Values.

Keypoints: Part 7

■ Leaders tend to make an assumption about human nature: they believe in the greatness that lies dormant within people.

■ If you trust people, you may on occasion be let down, but much more often people will respond in ways that fully justify your confidence.

■ Amazing things happen when you make people feel they are valued as individuals, when you treat them with dignity, when you show your respect for them by allowing them to exercise their own wisdom, judgement and discretion, when you invite them to be creative and to use their initiative.

■ Great people deserve great leaders. Your skilled leadership is a tribute you bring to the greatness of spirit of those you are privileged to serve.

■ The avowed intention to rely upon people having such qualities as humour and good faith unless they prove otherwise works wonders. It brings character and dignity to any organization.

Truth However Disenchanting Is Better
Than Falsehood However Comforting

Trust Only Those Who Have The Courage
To Contradict You With Respect
And Who Value Your Character
More Than Your Favour

An Ideal Is Often But A Flaming Vision Of Reality

Part 8

The Why Question

'Already we have explored a large territory,' began the young chief executive, 'and I am aware that I now have to put it all into practice in the next five years. My concern at the moment is whether or not I shall be able to remember it all! I know that I shall have the Keypoints to refresh my memory, but I need something like the Three-Circle Model which I can keep in mind and turn to in times of perplexity.' He stood up and drawing the model on the flip chart began to contemplate it, almost as if he had never seen it before.

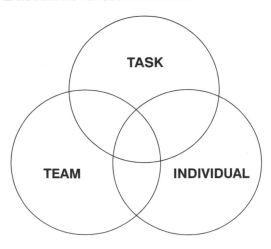

'As the Chinese proverb says, *A picture is worth a thousand words*,' I said, interrupting his thoughts. 'Yet, why should we multiply those few essential pictures or frameworks already in use? Perhaps we may find that the simple model of the Three Circles has enough depth for our purposes. For being simple should not be confused with being simplistic or superficial. Take the TASK circle, how do you see that now?'

'My job is clearly to set – or perhaps I should say identify – a series of challenging or demanding tasks. They must not be impossible, but on the other hand they have to stretch the individual, the team or the organization as a whole. And, of course, I have to persuade my operational and team leaders both to think like that and to have the art or skill to establish specific, time-bounded objectives that meet those criteria.'

'Yes, managers tend to focus far too much on the *measurability* of the task, in the fond belief that what you can measure you can manage or control. Leaders go beyond that basic need for concreteness or tangibility in their skill of pitching the task at the optimum level for engaging the human spirit.'

'Interesting,' commented the young chief executive, 'that using just the word TASK has already introduced a leadership element into the question. But you have reminded me, too, of another basic difference between managers, bosses or commanders – they tell you *what* to do, whereas leaders tell you *why* to do it. At that New York seminar the speaker said that CEOs should be like evangelists, going about the organization imparting their vision and their values. Shout the message loud and long enough and everyone eventually gets it. In that way you become a transformational leader.'

'I hope I have saved you from that fate,' I said. 'For the behaviour recommended is rather condescending, isn't it? If you have great people working in your organization, they know those things already. All that they need is an occasional quiet reminder, perhaps indirectly, that you know they know *why* the work is important or worthwhile. And, as Leonardo da Vinci once said:

He Who Truly Knows
Has No Occasion To Shout

'So if they don't know *why* the work matters – if, in other words, they lack a sense of purpose – we shouldn't be employing them?'

'That is so. It is a principle that great military leaders have understood since the days of Gideon. Oliver Cromwell expressed it best: *Give me the russet-coated captain who knows what he is fighting for and loves what he knows.*'

'In my business it is essential to create a delighted customer, and we can only do that on the quality, price and delivery of our goods and services.'

'And doubtless you employ people who know that. They may disagree with you or each other on how best to do it, but that's a secondary matter. And because of their calibre you have no doubts either that they will rise to meet both the challenges and the exceptional tasks that present themselves in any field, for business can be very difficult.'

'You know them well,' smiled the young chief executive.

'Not personally, but I know that they are persons of spirit, that they are on tiptoe to use all the energy, talent and creativity within them. The only issue is whether or not they have great leaders.'

'So to be a great leader I have to show a group the PURPOSE behind the tasks, be it the daily tasks or routines, or those special tasks, the steps to change, that lead us to becoming better that you mentioned. That enables me to communicate on a different level with people who already implicitly know that purpose.'

The Key of Morale

'That takes me to the TEAM circle,' continued the young chief executive. 'What stands out to me much more clearly is the importance of not just *teamwork* but also *team spirit*. The spirit of a group seems to have all the characteristics of an individual's spirit but writ large.'

'Yes, it's what the French call *esprit de corps* – that common spirit animating the members of a group and inspiring enthusiasm, devotion and a strong regard for the honour of the group. Another word borrowed from French is *morale*, which covers the mental, emotional and spiritual attitude of an individual, group or organization to the function or tasks expected of it. Both words suggest that sense of common purpose, that spiritual directed energy, that we touched upon earlier. To that we have to add another essential ingredient: confidence in the future.'

'You said that one of the seven generic functions of strategic leadership is to release this corporate spirit into the organization, but *how* do I go about it?'

'First, be aware of that corporate spirit – look at the symptoms or outward signs. For good or bad morale talks to you as a leader in the language of symptoms. Then, like a good doctor, all you have to do is remove the blocks or impediments that are preventing the greatness that is there from making its appearance. If you want glory, clean the windows.'

What Motivates Individuals

'The individual circle used to be populated in my mind by Maslow's Hierarchy of Needs – Physiological, Safety, Social, Self-Esteem and Self-Actualization,' said the young chief executive.

'And now?'

'I don't see people anymore as self-centred beings intent on meeting their own needs, be they the "lower" ones or some form of self-fulfilment or self-realization.'

'There is certainly quite a lot of *self* in all those words and concepts,' I said, with a smile. 'Like you, I cannot believe that we are quite so self-preoccupied. But aren't our needs the key to motivation? I know that it is now the dominant way of expressing it, but the more I think about it the less adequate it seems. Once I acted as consultant to an organization in Dubai. Itinerant workers from 15 different countries were engaged upon a major harbour-building project. The chief executive did some research and discovered that the common factor among them was their love for their families – the desire to do what our grandfathers used to call *bettering themselves*, to give their children better opportunities. It led me to reflect that love is the force that drives us – love of ourselves first...'

'But surely self-love is a bad thing?'

'You may be confusing it with selfishness, the state of being concerned excessively or exclusively with oneself, so that one concentrates on one's own advantage, pleasure or well-being without regard for others. Grasping greediness is always ugly. But that is quite different from having a sensible regard for one's own happiness or advantage. Is it also not against the tenet of self-love to aspire to use one's talents to the full, or to enjoy what recognition comes our way? We are told to love our neighbour *as ourselves*, which means to seek their good as we naturally do for ourselves.

'Secondly, love of family is very powerful. The most immediate and natural senses of the word *love* relate to the attachments of family. For most of us the "nuclear family" is the epicentre of widening concentric rings of attachment. And, as the psychologist C A Mace noted, *The radiant warmth of the human heart varies with the sum of the social difference.*

'Another natural love that motivates us stems from our social nature, the love of belonging. The love of the particular group or team, even the organization itself, can be as powerful as the love of family. Sometimes it is not the cause that keeps the soldier from running away but a resolve not to let down comrades who have never let him down. Patriotism, love for one's country, is a wider form of our capacity to love those social groupings to which we belong, ones that inspire our devotion.'

'With the environment under such threat, isn't there another love motivating us now: a love for the whole human race on earth and for this precious blue planet that is our common home?'

'I hope so. The equivalent of national selfishness is still a world problem and will be for years to come, but millions of people are now quietly coming to think of themselves primarily as human beings; members of the human race and – in Socrates' phrase – *citizens of the world*. Only secondarily do they see themselves as nationals of this nation or that.'

'We are capable of loving ideals, too,' added the young chief executive. 'We have this remarkable capacity to love abstract things, such as honour, truth, kindness, goodness, beauty, excellence in all its forms. We love to create new things and to achieve things. So, in place of all those need-based psychological theories, I propose the love principle.'

'It may not make your fortune as a management guru,' I said with a smile, 'but it's a very interesting idea. By the way, you mentioned that we have a love to *create*. Creative thinking takes place in the minds of individuals, but it takes a team to *innovate* – that is, to develop the individual's creative idea and eventually to bring it to the marketplace in the form of a new product or service.'

The Inspired Moment

'So the Three-Circle Model still serves, but the level of understanding and engagement has to be deeper?'

'That is how I see it. A leader with such a deep understanding – however intuitive – will be able to sense the *inspired moment*, that window of opportunity that opens up briefly where, if he or she does or says the right thing, the switch is thrown on the electrical circuit and that spiritual energy kicks in that enables people to transcend their previous limits or the ordinary levels of performance in a given field. Speaking from personal experience, those are moments you will remember all your life.'

'Do they transform or change you?'

'I wouldn't say that, but they take you a step or two closer to humility. Contrary to popular belief, it is not things that humiliate you – the failures, the insults, the misfortunes, the petty daily lacerations of the spirit that make you humble, though they have a part to play. No it is the sense of greatness in others and the realization that occasionally you have been the catalyst for locating, releasing and channelling that greatness. All have shared in an experience of glory. It may fade, but it leaves a glow behind.'

Keypoints: Part 8

■ Commanders and managers tell people what to do and, if they are wise, leave them as far as possible to decide when, who and where. Leaders also do that, but in addition they answer the why question in a way that satisfies the mind and lifts the spirit.

■ Leaders sometimes use indirect ways to communicate their sense of purpose. The most important thing is to be clear in your own mind as to what is the compelling purpose of the work you are doing.

■ All groups and organizations have a spirit, often only revealed in adversity. The chief expression of that spirit is 'high morale' – the determined and infectious attitude the team or organization shows towards accomplishing the common task in the teeth of difficulty.

■ Individuals are not predominantly motivated to meet their own lower or higher needs, as was previously thought. It is true that creating successful teams, achieving ambitious goals and doing good work all meet personal needs at various levels. But what moves us more is love – love of self, love of family, love of social groups who makes us feel that we belong, love of creativity and achievement, love of great and noble causes. The satisfaction of our own higher needs is essentially a by-product.

■ A leader can sense 'the inspired moment' – that time when the right words or actions can trigger off a chain reaction that leads to sustained inspiration. Remember: *Not geniuses, but average men and women require profound stimulation, incentive towards creative effort, and the nurture of great hopes.*

A Leader Is Best When People Are Hardly Aware
Of His Or Her Existence...
Fail to Honour People, And They Will Fail To Honour You.
But Of A Good Leader, Who Speaks Little,
When The Task Is Accomplished, The Work Done,
The People Say, 'We Did This Ourselves'

Part 9

The Test of Leadership

'Who in your opinion are the greatest leaders?' asked the young chief executive.

'Those who undergo the severest tests and still stand their ground.'

'Then I am not sure I want to be one,' he laughed. 'Seriously, I expected you to name some names. Can you give me an example of what you have in mind?'

'Take belief in people. We agreed that good leaders are among those who have a high or positive view of human nature: they believe in the inherent goodness of people. Not as good as we might be. As someone wrote over the mirror in an Arizonan bar:

I ain't what I ought to be,

I ain't what I'm going to be,

But I ain't what I was!

'Despite seeing the ugly side of human nature, good leaders do not lose faith in the underlying goodness within us. In *Long Road to Freedom* (1994), Nelson Mandela writes:

Even in the grimmest times in prison, when my comrades and I were pushed to our limits, I would see a glimmer of humanity in one of the guards, perhaps just for a second, but that was enough to reassure me and keep me going. Man's goodness is a flame that can be hidden but never extinguished.'

'How about confidence in the successful achievement of the task?'

Dealers in Hope

'That too can be put to the test. When the *expectancy* of success suddenly falls or gradually fades – usually because of unpredictable forces coming into play – then it is important for the leader not to succumb to the temptation of despair. For if he or she does, it will spread like a forest fire throughout the organization.'

'What's the difference between *expectancy* and *hope*?'

'Expectancy implies a high degree of certainty about the positive outcome. Hope, by contrast, suggests little certainty but conveys a confidence or assurance in the possibility or an assurance that what one desires will happen. The important point is that while hope is still alive you are in with a chance. As Alexander Dubcek, leader of the Czech uprising against the Russians, said: *Hope dies last; the person who loses hope also loses the sense of his future.*'

'So when things are going badly, professionally or personally, are you saying that it is important to maintain a climate of hope; it optimizes your (dwindling) chances of success?'

'Precisely. If these are the circumstances, then I would agree with J W Gardner that *a prime function of a leader is to keep hope alive*. It can be tough, but, as you rightly say, realistic hope does optimize what is left of your chance of winning. One of the advantages of experience is that you discover that even the darkest situations will sometimes change for the better. So leaders can sometimes steady those who confuse a failure or setback in life with total defeat. Charles M Schultz, creator of the *Peanuts* comic strip, expressed it well:

> There is one thing that I learned a long time ago... If you can hang on for a while longer, there is always something bright around the corner, or the dark clouds will go away and there will be some sunshine again if you are able to hold out. I think you just have to wait it out.

'It can be a long wait, however, and then the primal function of a leader is to keep hope alive. Once people fall into the clutches of Giant Despair, then morale has a habit of collapsing.'

'It must be very difficult to keep hope alive when one faces unbroken defeats or failures, when the dark clouds just get blacker and look more threatening.'

The Only Way To Lead Is To Show People The Future.
A Leader Is A Dealer In Hope

'But we are not talking here about just positive thinking or mere optimism, are we?' continued the young chief executive.

'No, optimism isn't quite the right word. For optimism is a temperamental inclination to look on the bright side and – unchecked by *realism* – it can be quite misleading. For example, a lifelong heavy smoker who happens to be an optimist, may be over-confident that he or she will avoid all the self-inflicted ills that come in the wake of his or her addiction.'

'What happens when even the rational grounds for hope begin to disappear and the future starts to disappear down the plughole?'

'It depends on the circumstances, but if a *particular* hope is extinguished, the more *general* hope may yet survive. If the cause is a great and noble one, for example, the hope remains that success will come in the long run, perhaps decades or even centuries hence.'

'Why do leaders believe that?' asked the young chief executive.

'Well, all great and good causes are related; they sink or swim together. Eventually, good is destined to triumph, though perhaps not in the way we envisage it. Meanwhile we are like soldiers fully engaged:

> For the cause that lacks assistance
> For the wrong that needs resistance
> For the future in the distance
> And the good that I can do.'

A Faith for Leaders

'That sounds like an act of faith to me,' commented the young chief executive.

'It is the faith you will find in a true leader. In Ordway Tead's *The Art of Leadership* (1935), a book my father gave me when I was a boy, the author defines a leader's faith as "*an active effort to bring good to pass based on the confirming experience that such activity is and does good.*" He continues:

> Fundamentally, a deeper kind of faith seems also invaluable if not essential. It may be called a spiritual faith. The words are not popular today because they are so often used as a cloak for lazy thinking and as implying an indiscriminately optimistic feeling about life – one which is grounded in no deep experience or justified by no tested convictions. There is, nevertheless, a permissible even if non-rational belief, by whatever name it is called, that the enterprise of living has a meaning and values which are precious, permanent and not at odds with the larger processes of the universe.

'It is that strategic hopefulness, that faith in the inevitable victory of the good, that gives leaders their confidence in facing the tactical difficulties of their own time and place.

'Take Dag Hammarskjöld as an example. As Secretary-General of the United Nations, the second to hold that office, he was the leader in the efforts to maintain peace in a world divided into Western and Eastern blocs. As the vision of a higher form of international society after the trauma of the Second World War, a new order of peace, seemed doomed, Hammarskjöld refused to abandon hope: "Sometimes that hope – the hope for that kind of reaction – is frustrated," he said, "*but it is a hope which is undying.*" His tragic death in an air-crash, while on his way to ceasefire talks with President Tshombe of Katanga during the Congo crisis in 1961, caused a sense of shock throughout the world.'

'Hope that is undying, "hope springs eternal in the human heart",' mused the young chief executive. 'But isn't it only rational to abandon hope when there are no longer any rational grounds for it?'

'No, hopes may dwindle from a torrent to a trickle, even a few drops. But when every hope is gone for you personally, you needn't give up hope. For hope is part of the human spirit, as essential to it as oxygen is to the body. If there is no one around you to love, it doesn't mean that love cannot live within you. Why give up hope because there is nothing to hope for? It is part of the essential you. G K Chesterton once said that anyone can hope when things look really hopeful. It is only when everything is hopeless that hope begins to be a strength at all. Like all the spiritual virtues, he added, *hope is as unreasonable as it is indispensable.*'

Keypoints: Part 9

■ All leaders will be tested, by loneliness if by no greater force. The greatest leaders are those who undergo the most severe trials but do not abandon their values or allow affliction to dim their spirits.

■ Leaders are 'dealers in hope', but they have to be honest brokers. It is counterproductive to paint unrealistic and rosy pictures about the future, worse to lie about it. A good leader is neither an optimist nor a pessimist, more a realist with an unconquerable hope.

■ Leadership is about creating and maintaining a climate of hope, one that makes success possible. Wise leaders know that fortunes can change, they know how to wait it out.

■ 'I do accept that I am a worm,' said Winston Churchill, but, he added with a chuckle, 'I do believe I am a glow worm.' Humility is important, not least because we grow by taking on board critical feedback. But each of us has a light for the path, a light to lead by.

■ In that dimly sensed conflict between good and evil the only thing we know intuitively for certain is that good is destined to win. That is why hope is underlying in the human spirit.

Towards Excellence

'I suppose that if you are going to grow in wisdom you need the humility to learn from others,' reflected the young chief executive.

'Yes, your teachers are all around you, not least at work or in your family. At the right time and place you must be open to what they really think of your leadership. As Francis Crick said, *Politeness is the poison of all good collaboration*, but most of us are too well mannered to be impolite to one another. In our culture rudeness tends simply to offend. What is needed is not rudeness so much as the more effective giving and receiving of feedback – information about the mutual effect you are having on others and they on you.'

'Yes, and in addition to feedback, I need also some opportunities to reflect and talk about leadership and management with others, preferably in other fields as well as business, so that I can build on the wisdom I have, such as it is. I don't suppose anyone ever improves in a sport, art or business unless they talk about it with their colleagues, do they?'

'Not to my knowledge,' I said.

The young chief executive closed his notebook and we had some coffee together.

'I have greatly enjoyed our conversations,' he said. 'What I feel I have been able to do is to put together my own philosophy or framework. Now I shall have to put it to the test.

'Whether I succeed or not remains to be seen, but I shall do my best. I know that I have a long way to go and it won't be easy, but I shall strive for excellence in leadership for the rest of my days. For at some point in our conversations a flame ignited within my mind, something I know will always burn bright or rekindle unless I grossly neglect it. I call it the spirit of leadership.'

'Well,' I said to him, as he stood up to go, 'you have fallen in love with a hard task-master, one who will ever be whispering in your ear *Don't spare yourself.* Only those who are demanding of themselves can inspire great things in others. It is a thought captured in a prayer of St Augustine of Hippo, a prayer for all who, like you, aspire to be good leaders and leaders for good:

> *To My God,*
> *A Heart Of Flame;*
> *To My Fellow Human Beings,*
> *A Heart Of Love;*
> *To Myself,*
> *A Heart Of Steel*

Notes and References

2   John Collier

8   Zulu proverb

9   Ralph Waldo Emerson

17 William Shakespeare in *King Lear*

17 Dag Hammarskjöld

37 J W Fortescue, writing on Wellington

44 The University of Cambridge orator speaking of General Eisenhower, Supreme Allied Commander in the invasion of Europe, on the occasion when he received an honorary degree.

51 Elbert Hubbard

55 Herman Melville

64 Antoine de Saint-Exupéry

69 Jan R Jonassen, *Leadership: Sharing the passion* (Management Pocket Books, Alresford, Hampshire)

72 William Blake

76 John Steinbeck

78 John Donne

78 Lord John Hunt, leader of the first expedition to climb Mount Everest in 1953.

80 Anonymous

86 Anonymous

92 Walt Whitman

95 Written by a Swedish manager and quoted in Richard Oliver, *Inspirational Leadership: Henry V and the muse of fire* (2001)

96 Bill Newman, *The Ten Laws of Leadership* (BNC, Brisbane, 1993)

99 Anonymous

102 Jan R Jonassen, *Leadership: Sharing the passion* (Management Pocket Books, Alresford)

103 Johann Goethe

109 John Buchan in 'Montrose and Leadership', a lecture given at the University of St Andrews, 27 January 1930

113 Emerson

116 Paul Gauguin, quoted by Henri Perruchot in his biography of the artist

118 Albert Schweitzer

118 François de Fenelon

118 Joseph Conrad

121 Leonardo da Vinci

128 Lao Tzu

132 Napoleon Bonaparte

138 St Augustine of Hippo

Solution to puzzle on p. 112

Source: Open University

Index

Don't let anyone tell you that the world is flat

www.koganpage.com

Fresh thinking for business today